ROUGH IN BRUTAL PRINT

Frail shadow of a woman in the flesh,
These very eyes of mine saw yesterday,
Would I re-tell this story of your woes,
Would I have heart to do you detriment
By pinning all this shame and sorrow plain
To that poor *chignon*,—staying with me still,
Though form and face have well-nigh faded now,—
But that men read it, rough in brutal print,
As two years since some functionary's voice
Rattled all this—and more by very much—
Into the ear of vulgar Court and Crowd?

Red Cotton Night-Cap Country, 2:679–89 (Browning apostrophizing Mme Debacker [Clara de Millefleurs], as he recalls an occasion on which he encountered her in the course of a stroll through Tailleville)

Rough
in Brutal Print

The Legal Sources of Browning's

Red Cotton Night-Cap

Country

Mark Siegchrist

OHIO STATE UNIVERSITY PRESS : COLUMBUS

Library of Congress Cataloguing in Publication Data

Siegchrist, Mark, 1944–
Rough in brutal print.

Includes bibliographical references and index.
1. Browning, Robert, 1812–1889. Red cotton
night-cap country—Sources. 2. Law in literature.
3. Caen (France)—Biography. 4. Mellerio family.
5. Mellerio, Antonio, 1827–1870. 6. Debacker,
Anna Sophie Trayer, 1830–1887. I. Title
PR4222.R353S55   821′.8   81-3993
    ISBN 0-8142-0327-2   AACR2

For my mother

CONTENTS

CONTENTS

Acknowledgments

I am grateful to everyone who helped in the preparation of this small study, and I would especially like to thank the following for their various kindnesses:

Agnes Scott College, for a grant for the summer of 1972 for travel to Normandy to obtain the documents;

Huguette Kaiser, professor of French at Agnes Scott College, for her diplomatic tact in dealing with the French bureaucracy;

Louis Bolloc'h, Procureur de la République, Tribunal de Grande Instance de Caen, and Gildas Bernard, Directeur des Services d'Archives du Calvados, for making the original documents available for study;

the University of Caen, for permission to use the library;

François Mellerio, of the Mellerio-Meller jewelry firm in Paris, for allowing me to examine their privately printed family history;

Jack W. Herring, director of the Browning Armstrong Library at Baylor University, for providing the *Journal de Caen* text of the 1873 appeal from the Meynell Collection;

Roma King, professor of English at Ohio University, for his generosity in sharing the results of his own work with the *Journal de Caen* article on the 1873 appeal;

Brigitte Coste, assistant professor of French in the Department of Foreign Languages at Marquette University, for her linguistic finesse;

Michael K. McChrystal, assistant dean of the Marquette University Law School, for his expertise in "terms of art";

and Carol Worm, whose typing skills are as extraordinary as her patience.

ROUGH IN BRUTAL PRINT

Advertisement

I premise, and wish to have distinctly borne in mind by any reader of this poem, that it is no more nor less than a mere account treated poetically, of certain problematic facts taken just as I find them given, by parties to a dispute, in the published pleadings of their respective legal advocates and the formal decision of a Court of Law. Each and every such statement, therefore, affecting the conduct of either party, must be considered as depending absolutely upon public authority and pretending to no sort of guarantee for its truth obtainable from private sources of information—into none of which have I the will or power to enquire. My business confines itself to working a sum from arbitrary or imaginary figures: if these be correct, the result should follow as I give it—not otherwise. Nor would I attempt the working at all, had not the parties themselves begun by proposing the figures for examination. No fact has been purposely changed, although conversations, declared and described, could only be re-produced by a guess at something equivalent. Either party may—and one must have—exaggerated or extenuated or invented: my concern is exclusively with these presumable exaggerations and extenuations and inventions as they were presented to and decided upon by the Court of the Country, as they exist in print, and as they may be procured by anybody.

R. B.

(Letter to George Smith, Browning's publisher of *Red Cotton Night-Cap Country*, 8 March 1873, in *New Letters of Robert Browning*, ed. William Clyde DeVane and Kenneth Leslie Knickerbocker [New Haven, Conn.: Yale University Press, 1950], pp. 211–12. The editors remark that this paragraph is presumably an outline of Browning's "first defense against a libel action" [p. 211].)

1

Introduction

Although Browning wholeheartedly shared his public's admiration of *The Ring and the Book* (1868–69),[1] in all the twenty years—and fifteen volumes—that followed its publication only once more did he undertake the same sort of project as he had when he set out to resuscitate the *Old Yellow Book*. That poem was *Red Cotton Night-Cap Country* (1873), and although it deals with a local and contemporary French scandal instead of a remote seventeenth-century Italian crime, it closely resembles *The Ring and the Book* in its aim to bring out of a historical episode the full imaginative truth from beneath the surface of the public record. Both poems begin with legal transcripts as their raw material, and both are concerned to display the ability of unprejudiced sympathy to arrive at a more sensitive understanding of the actors' real motives than is possible for either the biased selfishness of interested witnesses or the impersonal machinery of institutionalized inquiry.

Consequently, in order to demonstrate this superior capacity of the imaginative vision as impressively as possible, both poems lay heavy stress on the extent of their reliance on publicly available testimony as well as on the strictness of their adherence to those directly reported facts. The twirling about of the *Old Yellow Book* by its cover and the verbatim quotation of evidence submitted to the French court are both dramatic gestures whose effect is to assure the reader that whenever he may come across occasional passages of interpretation in these poems he can rely on their being based solidly on the "pure crude fact"[2] of the actual events. Both these poems insist that their art is essentially not a fictional-

izing transformation of objective fact but rather a revivifica-
tion, a discovery of the original truth hidden beneath an ob-
scuring crust of documentation. The reiterated claims of each
of these works to full historical accuracy are important elements in determining the quality of a reader's response. Every observing eye must, of course, inevitably interpret what it
sees; nevertheless, for a reader to draw interpretation as hon-
estly as possible from a given set of historical data is undeniably a different sort of experience from drawing that interpretation from a set of fictions that he realizes has been
deliberately invented for the occasion. There is no question
here of making judgments about any type of inherent supe-
riority: the one set simply has a particular sense of being
grounded in a public reality that the other does not, and it
therefore elicits a different kind of response.

Much of the effectiveness of these two works, therefore,
depends on the completeness of the reader's confidence in
their factual accuracy, and thus they provide unusually op-
portune occasions to study the processes by which Browning
selected and arranged the material he chose as vehicles to
present his themes. Much of the interest of the studies by
Hodell and Gest, which compare the original material of the
Old Yellow Book with Browning's version of those documents in *The Ring and the Book*, lies in their discovery of a
far greater degree of discrepancy from that original material
than could possibly have been suspected from Browning's
repeated insistence within that poem on his faithful adherence to the details in his source.[3] These studies show clearly
that, once Browning had decided on what his own interpretation would be, he did not scruple to distort or even simply
to omit fragments of evidence that inconveniently did not
suggest the meaning he had decided that his murder story
should display. Any writer is, of course, perfectly free to do
whatever he pleases with his source material; but for Browning to have proclaimed his historical fidelity so loudly, while
covertly smudging so many recalcitrant details, demonstrates his awareness of how important that *impression* of
fidelity is to his themes, while it reveals to what an unsus-
pected degree that impression is actually the result of a deliberate distortion of raw material.

By way of sampling in *The Ring and the Book* the kinds and degrees of alteration and omission involved in what so strenuously purports to be an accurate transcription of historical fact, let us glance briefly at the information brought foward by Hodell and Gest. These critics show that in innumerable matters of detail—names, chronology, trifling facts of all kinds, verbatim citations, even down to occasional etymological echoes in vocabulary and construction in some of the closer paraphrases from the Italian (Hodell, *Source*, p. 257)—Browning was remarkably, even pedantically, faithful to his original. But in more substantive material he was found to have often deviated more or less widely from his insistently reiterated principles. For instance, we can grant that in such questions as the exact nature of the feelings between Pompilia and Caponsacchi, or in the attribution of Pompilia's sense of her impending motherhood as the immediate motive for her flight from Arezzo, Browning is justified in his claim that there is at least nothing in the evidence to contradict his interpretations (though there is also, it must be said, nothing whatever in the evidence to support them either). But it is startling to learn from these source studies, after reading in Browning's poem all those protestations of painstaking fidelity to fact, that it is quite clear from the *Old Yellow Book* not only that Pompilia certainly lied when she claimed to be unable to write, and when she claimed that she and Caponsacchi did not arrive at the inn at Castelnuovo until dawn, but that actually she lied pretty consistently throughout her entire deposition. This conclusion is the only inference that can fairly be drawn from the frequent discrepancies between her statement and Caponsacchi's (the two accused would have been interrogated separately), especially considering that, as A. K. Cook remarks in his *Commentary*, "When she and Caponsacchi differed as to facts his version is often supported by other evidence, but . . . hers is not."[4] And indeed, as Judge Gest observes in his admirably lucid analysis of the various depositions, "It cannot be said that the matters as to which [Pompilia and Caponsacchi] thus disagreed were non-essential details. They were the pivotal points of the case" (Gest, *Old Yellow Book*, p. 604). Most astonishing of all to a reader of *The Ring and the Book* is

Gest's later comment: "Upon all the facts as thus developed, it seems quite clearly established that Pompilia was guilty of adultery with Caponsacchi" (Gest, *Old Yellow Book*, p. 610). Cook, even though his attitude toward Browning is that of the adoring hero-worship found in so much turn-of-the-century critical literature, is reduced to musing, "It is a question of great interest how in the face of such discrepancies [Browning] could so greatly exaggerate his fidelity to his source"; he recovers his equanimity only by concluding that "an examination of the conflicting depositions can hardly fail . . . to add immensely to [our] admiration of Browning's genius. It will show [us] that he picked and chose *and altered* with consummate skill" (Cook, *Commentary*, p. 292, italics mine). Considerations of space preclude listing them here, but there are literally dozens of matters of fact, of both lesser and greater significance, that Browning decided either to alter or silently to eliminate in order to make plausible his transformation of the shabby moral ambiguities of the *Old Yellow Book* into the ideal heroisms and villainies of *The Ring and the Book*. Three years later, he once again engaged in much the same sort of creative process in the composition of *Red Cotton Night-Cap Country*. This present study, in making available the original sources of this later poem, Browning's only other excursion into large-scale historical transcription, thus offers the only other available opportunity for insight into his aims and methods in such an undertaking.

Before proceeding with a description of those sources, it may be helpful to provide a brief summary of the events exactly as they appear in Browning's poem, so as to have a clear basis of comparison with the material in the original documents. For the benefit of those readers whose recollection of *Red Cotton Night-Cap Country* is not as fresh as it might be, this review will take the form of a short synopsis of each of the four books of the poem, each part comprised of roughly one thousand lines of blank verse. To avoid subsequent confusion, I will use the original names throughout, not the metrical equivalents Browning substituted in his final draft to avoid a possible libel suit (such as "la Ravissante" for "la

Délivrande," "Clara de Millefleurs" for "Anna de Beaupré," and so on.

Most of book one is devoted to a circuitous arrival at the subject of the poem's narrative. The scene opens with a gentleman chatting casually with a lady friend as they stroll through the countryside near Saint Aubin on the Norman coast. (Circumstantial detail scattered through the poem shows clearly that these two figures must be Browning and Miss Anne Thackeray.) This first portion of the poem lays great stress on the quietness of the scene, a somnolence so pervasive that Miss Thackeray is moved to offer her sobriquet, taken from the traditional headgear of the local peasantry, "White Cotton Night-Cap Country." In a spirit of playful rivalry, Browning then rouses himself to recall some episode or other that has occurred in this apparently peaceful place that will be sufficiently terrible, or at least dramatic, that Miss Thackeray will then be forced to concede that "Red Cotton Night-Cap Country" would after all be the more appropriate name. "Red" and "white" are thus established as symbols of a sense of moral polarity running throughout the poem, in conjunction with the theme that, to a sharp and sympathetic eye, there is always much to be discovered beneath a public surface:

> The proper service every place on earth
> Was framed to furnish man with [is] . . .
> To give him note that, through the place he sees,
> A place is signified he never saw,
> But, if he lack not soul, may learn to know.
>
> (1.60–64)

Placed on his mettle, then—"forward, the firm foot! / Onward, the quarry-overtaking eye!" (1.399–400)—Browning rambles on and on about the passing highlights of the local scenery until his eye is caught by the church tower of la Délivrande, which reminds him of last week's ceremony of coronation for its famous statue of the Virgin, which reminds him of the gems donated for the occasion by the wealthy Parisian jeweler Mellerio, whose country château the speaker and his friend are now approaching—and he finds that he has suddenly and inadvertently discovered his "tragic bit of

Red" (1.732). Not yet betraying the full melodramatic scarlet of Mellerio's story, Browning begins by sketching in how the Mellerio family had grown rich from their fashionable jewelry firm in Paris, and how Antonio Mellerio had decided some years back to retire from the Parisian social whirl to this Norman château with his beloved wife (as she is referred to at this point in the poem [1.722]), to devote his life to charitable works. In response to Miss Thackeray's skepticism that anything very terrible can be found in what will no doubt prove to be merely the usual story of rural domestic ennui, Browning sits her down with a flourish in front of the château's gay façade, "One laugh of color and embellishment" (1.1020), informs her that it was on this very spot that two years ago "tragic death befell" (1.1023), and starts to tell her the lurid tale in full detail.

Book two begins with three hundred lines that give a general characterization of Mellerio as an unstable mixture of emotional sweetness, loose sexual morality, superstitious religious faith, and dim intellect. It is here that Browning first introduces the elaborate "Turf and Towers" symbolism of the poem's subtitle, a recurring emblem through whose variations Browning will display the course of Mellerio's continuing struggle to reconcile the rival claims of "Faith's tower" (2.270) and the "daisy-dappled turf" (2.274) of sensual pleasure:

> Keep this same
> Notion of outside mound and inside mash,
> Towers yet intact round turfy rottenness,
> Symbolic partial-ravage,—keep in mind!
>
> (2.114–17)

Browning's portrait of Mellerio shows him to have been "impenetrably circuited" (2.141) by an orthodox Catholic faith in his childhood, and then to have turned as a youth to unrestrained romantic "sport" (2.362). After some years of dissipation had passed, at the age of twenty-five he encountered at the theater the beautiful Mme Debacker, who then called herself Anna de Beaupré and who told him the "preliminary lie" (2.627) that she came from a poor but noble family and had just returned from an unsuccessful attempt at a stage career in London. Only after Mellerio's affections were fully secured did she eventually tell him the more sordid truth, which was that as a mere nobody from Metz she had come to Paris to become a milliner, had married a young tailor who had taken her to London to try their commercial fortune, and had fled back alone to Paris after M. Debacker had had the effrontery to try to "traffic in his wife" (2.647). In Browning's poem Mme Debacker appears to have been at this time nothing better than a concubine, maintained in luxury by a series of wealthy patrons. Mellerio, mistaking this exotic hothouse polyanthus for a simple primrose, as he also mistook cross superstititon for true spirituality, fell hopelessly in love with her. After enduring a number of difficult events, including the deaths of his father and beloved brother, and a socially embarrassing suit for separation brought by M. Debacker, who had by now prospered as a tailor and wished to secure himself against a possible claim by his wife of her fair share of their marital goods, Mellerio and Mme Debacker left the running of the jewelry shop to his cousins and retired to the rural seclusion of his family's château in Tailleville, on the Norman coast. Although under the circumstances they could not marry, they settled down in every other respect to a circumspect and regular life, redecorating the château in rococo elegance at vast expense, inviting friends to visit from Paris, and quietly enjoying each other's company. Browning compares this stage of Mellerio's career to a wilfully blind effort to entrench himself in a pavilion, a "temporary tent" (2.1080) within which he could safely ignore the "dim grim outline of the circuit-wall" (2.1081) of towers, with its uncompromising call to strict religious morality. "And so slipt pleasantly away five years / Of Paradisiac dream" (3.1–2).

Book three presents the gradual collapse of that dream. It opens with Mellerio's being summoned to Paris one winter, to face his adored mother's remonstrances concerning his lavish expenses and his "reprehensible illicit bond" (3.51). Bitterly stung by remorse, Mellerio then threw himself into the Seine. He barely survived the subsequent fever, and in that condition of severe weakness, both physical and mental, he was called back once more to Paris only two months later, to

11

bear the sudden shock of his dear mother's death. The family ruthlessly pressed Mellerio, now heir to a substantial portion of the immense jewelry fortune, to abandon Mme Debacker, claiming that Mme Mellerio had died of a broken heart caused by her son's continued immoral behavior. "You hardly wonder if down fell at once / The tawdry tent . . . / And showed the outer towers distinct and dread" (3.269–70, 274). This time, Mellerio's feelings of guilt were so intense that a week after his mother's burial he was discovered kneeling at a fireplace, holding in the flames a crystal casket containing his letters from Mme Debacker, chanting, "Burn, burn and purify my past!" (3.426). By the time he was dragged away from the fire, he had burned his hands off to the wrists. In a fit of penitence he swore to leave Mme Debacker and return to a life of exemplary respectability, but no sooner had be begun to recover his health than he tottered back to Mme Debacker, sold his share of the jewelry business to his cousins, and returned to the château at Tailleville for good. There he had artificial hands of hard rubber fitted for his wrists, learned to write and even paint with his mouth, and for the next two years led as normal a life as possible under the circumstances, displaying an increasingly extraordinary generosity to the nearby church of la Délivrande.

Book four opens on a bright spring morning, 20 April 1870, with Mellerio about to set out for a ride on a colt that needed breaking in. While the grooms prepared the animal's equipment, Mellerio bounded up the stairs to the belvedere of the château, to pass the time by surveying the weather on the horizon. At this point occurs the poem's thematic core, a long and brilliant dramatic monologue "in Browning's finest manner,"[5] according to Philip Drew, delivered by Mellerio from the top of his belvedere. Addressing a review of his life to the Virgin of la Délivrande, Mellerio gradually comes to see clearly for the first time that, for all his agonizings of conscience, he has never been able to muster an absolute faith in the Virgin's power and her mercy. As his fervor increases, he seeks "to prove [his] indubitable faith" (4.264), asking, "What act shall evidence sufficiency / Of faith" (4.222–23), a "Faith [so] without flaw" (4.268) that it will move the Virgin to perform some miracle so astonishing that it will not only redeem his life with Mme Debacker but that the news of it will regenerate all France as well? Recalling the old tale that the statue of the Virgin of la Délivrande had originally been carried by angels to the very spot where they wished the church to be built, he leaps over the balustrade of the belvedere in full confidence that the Virgin will enable him to fly safely from his château to her church.

> A sublime spring from the balustrade
> About the tower so often talked about,
> A flash in middle air, and stone-dead lay
> [Antonio Mellerio] on the turf.
>
> (4.338–41)

Given all the facts as he set them down, even considering what he sees as Mellerio's foolish superstitiousness, Browning characteristically approves the wholeheartedness with which Mellerio finally acted to claim what he at last had decided was his life's ultimate good. "And I advise you imitate this leap, / Put faith to proof, be cured or killed at once!" (4.355–56). The rest of the story is dénouement. When the cousins appeared in smug confidence that Mellerio's fortune was now securely theirs, safe from the grasping adventuress, Mme Debacker greeted them with the news that Mellerio had left all his enormous estate to la Délivrande, except for a life estate in the château and an annual income for herself. The cousins then claimed that his death had been suicide, and brought suit to overthrow the bequests on the grounds of insanity. But the court judged that, although Mellerio had undoubtedly been eccentric and "Exuberant in generosities" (4.951), there was no evidence of suicide; and besides, in spite of all their accusations, the cousins had considered him perfectly sane enough to do business with when they had seen advantage to themselves in purchasing his share of the jewelry firm. Browning's summary of the court's judgment ends:

> " . . . no fact confirms the fear
> He meditated mischief to himself
> That morning when he met the accident
> Which ended fatally. The case is closed."
>
> (4.952–55)

The poems ends with a twenty-line coda, in which Brown-

13

ing asks Miss Thackeray, as he finishes composing his work,
if he has not made good his promise of that previous summer
in Normandy to make her a poem out of "All this poor story
[that he had then told her on the beach]—truth and nothing
else" (4.982).

Browning was, as usual, full of enthusiasm for his latest
work, but on this occasion he "was very doubtful as to its
reception by the public,"[6] and rightly so. Almost to a person,
the contemporary reviewers were dismayed by what they saw
as its quite perverse degree of difficulty. The writer for
Harper's, for instance, called it "quite as obscure and per-
plexing in its twisted and tortured sentences as anything
[Browning] has ever written," and he went on to defend his
failure even to read it all through on the grounds that "it is
not necessary to traverse every square mile of the Great Desert
to know that its scenery is tame."[7] However, impenetrable as
many of them found it, some reviewers did at least manage
vaguely to perceive, and generally to admire, Browning's effort "to get out of the ideal medium altogether into the actual
workaday world."[8] The *British Quarterly Review* approved:
"Our interest in this story is maintained by our being led
perforce to trace the process by which the poet finds in what
seem the most perverted elements the dim reflex of high possibilities, ruined by admixture of incompatible qualities of
temperament."[9] William Dean Howells, on the other hand,
in the *Atlantic Monthly*, was so outraged by a poem "as
unhandsome as it is unwholesome" that he found it finally
defensible "neither as a lesson from a miserable fact, nor as a
successful bit of literary realism."[10]

Thirty years later, in a discussion of *Red Cotton Night-
Cap Country* leading to the judgment that it is, "if . . . not
absolutely one of the finest of Browning's poems, . . . certainly one of the most magnificently Browningesque," G. K.
Chesterton observed that "it is worth noting that Browning
was one of those wise men who can perceive the terrible and
impressive poetry of the police-news, which is commonly
treated as vulgarity, which is dreadful and may be undesira-
ble, but is certainly not vulgar."[11] More recent commentary
has also tended to find at least part of the poem's value in its
transformation of tawdry fact into significant meaning, with

Philip Drew, for example, assigning it to "a place among the best Victorian long poems," and including the following remarks in his consideration:

> From this unpromising material, the very stock-in-trade of the sensational journalist, Browning made his peom. He retained the actual names of the participants and made virtually no alteration in the story: indeed the whole affair was so readily recognizable that Browning felt it expedient to substitute fictious names while the poem was in proof in order to avoid a possible action for libel.
>
> The incidents themselves being given in this way, the main interest of the poem lies in Browning's narrative technique and in his problings for the motives of the characters involved. The comparison with *The Ring and the Book* is obvious. . . .

Later, Drew observes of the closing portion of the poem, after Mellerio's death, that "what follows is all very well done-. . . but the effect is necessarily one of anti-climax: these incidents are included in the story not because they are required for its artistic completeness but because they actually happened, because the poem claims to be 'Truth and nothing else' " (Drew, *Poetry of Browning*, pp. 340, 322, 328–29). Clyde de L. Ryals's concluding comment in his study of the poem is, "It is a mark of Browning's genius that he could make out of this material, which basically is that of a naturalistic novel, an intriguing and ultimately delightful philosophical poem" (Ryals, *Browning's Later Poetry*, p. 100). There is, by the way, on this subject of his continuing penchant for "naturalistic" subjects, an illuminating remark from Browning himself, in a letter to Julia Wedgwood dated 19 November 1868, in defensive reply to her objection that she found the subject matter of *The Ring and the Book* to be painfully sordid. In this letter Browning is, of course, referring to his treatment of the Roman murder story, but, given the number of close technical and thematic similarities between the two works, his comments apply equally well to *Red Cotton Night-Cap Country*:

> I believe I do unduly like the study of morbid cases of the soul,—and I will try and get over that taste in future works; because, even if I still think that mine was the proper way to treat this particular subject,—the objection still holds, "Why

prefer this sort of subject?"—as my conscience lets me know I do.

Come, next time I will try in other directions. [Browning was for a short while as good as his word, in *Balaustion's Adventure* (1871), and possibly even in *Prince Hohenstiel-Schwangau* (1871), though he sadly backslid in his next two works, *Fifine at the Fair* (1872) and *Red Cotton Night-Cap Country* (1873).] But here,—given the subject, I cannot but still say, given the treatment too: the business has been, as I specify, to explain *fact*—and the fact is what you see and, worse, are to see. [At this point only the first half of *The Ring and the Book* had been published.] The question with me has never been "Could not one, by changing the factors, work out the sum to better result?," but declare and prove the actual result, and there an end. Before I die, I hope to purely invent something,—here my pride was concerned to invent nothing: the minutest circumstance that denotes character is *true*: the black is so much—the white, no more. You are quite justified perhaps in saying "Let all that black alone"—but, touching it at all, so much of it must be.[12]

Browning recounted his method of proceeding with the composition of *Red Cotton Night-Cap Country* in a letter to T. J. Nettleship, 16 May 1889, beginning with his first acquaintance with the tale of Mellerio's violent death:

I heard, first of all, the merest sketch of the story on the spot. Milsand told me that the owner of the house had destroyed himself from remorse at having behaved unfilially to his mother. In a subsequent visit (I paid one every year while Milsand lived there) he told me some other particulars, and they at once struck me as likely to have been occasioned by religious considerations as well as passionate woman-love,— and I concluded that there was no intention of committing suicide; and I said at once that I would myself treat the subject *just so*.

Afterward he procured me the legal documents. I collected the accounts current among the people of the neighborhood, inspected the house and grounds, and convinced myself that I had guessed rightly enough in every respect. Indeed the facts are so exactly put down, that, in order to avoid the possibility of prosecution for Libel—that is, telling the exact truth—I changed all the names of persons and places, as they stood in the original "Proofs," and gave them as they are to be found in Mrs. Orr's Hand-book. (*Letters of Robert Browning*, ed. Hood, p. 309)

Taking as a cue Browning's remark that "Milsand procured me all the essential documents" (*Letters of Robert Browning*, ed. Hood, p. 211), in 1972 I traveled to the Archives du Calvados in Caen, the city where the trial with which the poem deals had occurred exactly one hundred years ago. Although the old archives had been bombed in World War II, most of the material had been preserved in cellars around the city and had recently been transferred into a new facility. The documents available there included the handwritten copies of the original pleadings, the published records of the court's judgment, and several newspaper accounts, of which by far the most complete was that of *L'Ordre et la Liberté*. These are all translated in full in the following pages. The last phrase in the official record of the court's judgment was "Appeal by the Mellerio heirs"; investigation disclosed that in 1873, one year later, after the publication of Browning's poem, the Mellerios had indeed filed an appeal with the next higher court, the Cour d'Appel de Caen. The briefs, summary, newspaper accounts, and decision of that appeal were also on file in the Archives. After the discovery in the University of Caen of a short notice of the Mellerios' second and final appeal in 1874 to the Cour de Cassation, the highest court of appeal in France, there was nothing more to be found in Calvados except for some details on the subsequent history of the château from the mayor of Tailleville and the mother superior of the Convent of la Délivrande. In Paris the Mellerio family were kind enough to provide me with a family history that had been written by Joseph Mellerio, the cousin who had been most responsible for bringing the original suit against Mme Debacker. This volume contained an understandably biased account of the entire affair from the family's point of view, and also made possible a more exact identification of the various "Cousinry" mentioned in Browning's poem. Professor Roma King, of Ohio University, later generously offered his copies of a lengthy newspaper account of the 1873 appeal obtained from the Browning collection at Baylor University. Selections from this material, containing the most interesting of the new evidence and arguments, are included below in chapter 6.

The important question of exactly which of these documents were the ones Browning actually used cannot, I think, be decided conclusively. Obviously, all those documents relating to the two appeals are later than the writing of *Red Cotton Night-Cap Country*, and are therefore not relevant to this problem. They have the same corroborative interest for readers of this poem as the material in Beatrice Corrigan's *Curious Annals* has for readers of *The Ring and the Book*.[13] As for materials relating to the 1872 trial, there can be no question about the pleadings and the judgment, since they are the complete and original texts that must have been among the "legal documents" Browning obtained from Milsand. But the problem of finally determining which of the various newspaper accounts he may actually have consulted is probably insoluble. Of all the newspapers on file in the Archives, only *L'Ordre et la Liberté* gave a detailed day-by-day narration of the trial; for the 1873 appeal this paper was content with a single-issue summary—perhaps to avoid a boring redundancy, since much of the original trial material naturally reappears in the appeal. The account of the 1873 appeal on file at Baylor is that of the *Journal de Caen*, which provided for the appeal the same degree of detail as *L'Ordre et la Liberté* had for the 1872 trial, but I was unable to consult the 1872 volume of the *Journal de Caen* because the collection of that newspaper in the Archives dates back only to 1877. But both these publications have an air of solid respectability, in contrast to many others in the archives; and since there is no conflict in their versions of the appeal, it seems unlikely that there would be any significant conflict in their versions of the trial.

The question that remains is really one of what other information may have been available to Browning: for instance, he claims at various points in the course of the poem to be copying directly not only from evidence submitted in the trial but also from the records of the Convent of la Délivrande (3.883–916). Browning may have obtained this supplementary material from the mother superior of the Convent, "Nun I know" (3.867, 991); but when I visited the convent, the current mother superior informed me that she had no idea what documents Browning might be referring to. The result of this state of affairs, as regards a comparison of the poem with the source material, must therefore be, I think, that though firm conclusions about distortion on Browning's part can safely be drawn when his version actually contradicts the original documents translated here, he cannot necessarily be supposed to have invented in his occasional discussion of matter that does not appear in this collection. These source documents can also be used to follow the process by which Browning silently altered original data to suit his themes by distorting or simply omitting all kinds of conflicting evidence. He may well have felt it desirable to simplify the considerable complexity of the case; but by ignoring well over half the material in the trial, he often gives a very different slant on the personalities and issues involved, in spite of his repeated insistence on the thoroughness of his factual objectivity. Chapter five of this study presents a detailed examination of the major discrepancies between the source material and the poem that purportedly re-creates it so faithfully, together with a discussion of what light these discrepancies cast on the themes Browning had predetermined that his historical episode would reveal.

Finally, before turning to the documents themselves, it may be of some service to provide a brief survey of the rather tangled legal situation they deal with. In Browning's poem Mellerio is represented as having made only one testament (4.648–51), in which he left his entire estate to the Convent of la Délivrande, with a life estate to be held by Mme Debacker. That is, the estate would belong to the convent, but Mme Debacker would be entitled to the use of it during her lifetime. (Throughout this study the term *testament* will be used to refer to this type of legal document to avoid confusion with the term *will*—in the sense of *volition* or *will power*—which will occur frequently in discussions of the question of undue influence on Mellerio's possibly unsound mind.) In the poem Browning relates that the cousins simply brought suit for nullification of the testament on the grounds of Mellerio's unsoundness of mind, and lost. But the actual situation was much more complicated. In the five years before his death, Mellerio had drawn up no fewer than five testaments and an annuity:

1. 27 February 1865: 120,000 francs to Mme Debacker, the balance to his family (At this distance it is not possible to determine the exact equivalent of 1870 francs in 1980 dollars; but my sense of the amounts mentioned in various contexts in these documents is that the buying power of a franc at that time was roughly equal to two or three dollars in 1980, so 120,000 francs would have amounted to something like $300,000. The public prosecutor remarked that one of the reasons for the importance of this case was "the huge sums at stake.");

2. 6 January 1868: 150,000 francs to Mme Debacker, the balance to his family;

3. 4 June 1868: half the estate (an increment) to Mme Debacker, half to his family;

4. 17 September 1868: an annuity of 12,000 francs to Mme Debacker, beginning immediately;

5. 18 June 1869: the entire estate to Mme Debacker, with the property at Tailleville in life estate only, to be made after her death into a hospital for the maimed;

6. 21 October 1869: a more exact legal form of number five, giving Tailleville plus 200,000 francs to the Convent of la Délivrande after the death of Mme Debacker.

After Mellerio's death, on 13 April 1870, the suit brought by the cousins in fact contested the testament on two separate, though related, grounds: they charged not only that Mellerio's unsoundness of mind made him incompetent to make a valid testament but also that Mme Debacker and the Convent of la Délivrande had been in collusion to exert undue influence on Mellerio's weakened mind, coercing him into making a testament in their favor. Consequently, the case actually involved two charges, not just one, and three parties to the suit, not just two. And the suit itself did not directly aim at a flat nullification; instead, the heirs were trying to convince the court to order a commission of inquiry, in which, under French law, oral as well as written testimony could be given. There is no exact equivalent for this situation in American law. The attorney for the plaintiffs—the cousins—thus had the delicate problem of admitting that his case was not strong enough to argue for immediate nullification while insisting that nevertheless it was strong enough to warrant ordering a commission of inquiry, where his case would then be recognized as strong enough to compel nullification; the attorneys for the defense—Mme Debacker and the convent—had the equally delicate problem of seeking to deny the request for a commission of inquiry without seeming to be anxious to hide anything.

Because of the political upheavals of 1870 and 1871, the case did not come to trial before the summer of 1872. Actually, the term *trial* is only an approximate description of such a proceeding. Under French law, "in non-criminal actions, the word 'trial' is inappropriate; the securing of evidence, the development of the legal contentions, the definition of relevant issues, take place gradually over an extended period of time until the case is ready for final determination; the record so compiled is then submitted to the full court with oral argument."[14] In this case the process recorded in the newspaper accounts presented below is the oral argument accompanying the submission of the compiled record. It lasted three weeks, from 17 June to 8 July 1872, and in structure resembled a formal debate. The attorneys for the heirs, for Mme Debacker, and for the convent each took an uninterrupted turn presenting their side of the case, with the support of documentary evidence only, and then each took a turn at rebuttal. After the pleadings of each of the advocates, an impartial summary was made by the public prosecutor. Since this official has no exact counterpart in the American judicial system, the following description may help to clarify his prominent role in this case:

> Parallel to the hierarchy of the judges [in the French judiciary], there exists a hierarchy of public officials who are agents of the executive and yet, as part of the magistrature, are appointed and classified as judges. The office of *ministère public* originated in the fourteenth century. As in England, the king entrusted the presentation of his views on litigated matters of a public or general interest to a law-trained representative acting in his name. . . . The Revolutionary decrees formally recognized the officers of the *ministère public* as agents of the executive power before the courts. . . .

In the court of first instance [for example, in the 1872 trial], he is known as the *procureur de la République*; elsewhere [for example, in the 1873 appeal], as the *procureur général*. In criminal matters, the *ministère public* corresponds to the prosecutor or district attorney of Anglo-American law. In non-criminal court proceedings [such as the Mellerio affair], the *ministère public* represents societal or community interests in general . . . [and] may assume responsibility for the presentation [in pending cases] of independent arguments [that] carry greater weight with the judges than do those of private litigants.[14]

Although the Mellerio affair was not a criminal case, the title "public prosecutor" seems to me to convey successfully this official's function of representing an impartial public interest. (His own description of his duties in this particular case appears on p. 96.)

After the speech of the public prosecutor, the court handed down its judgment; and six months later, in January 1873, Browning finished his poem. In July 1873 the heirs filed their first unsuccessful appeal, and in August 1874 the Cour de Cassation struck down their second and final appeal. More than four years after Mellerio's death, Mme Debacker and the convent finally took clear title to the château of Tailleville.

One further note on discrepancies between the French and American legal systems may be useful: the notaries (*les notaires*) who appear so frequently in the following pages are far more important officials than are their counterparts in American or English society. In France

the *notaire* is a trained lawyer, completely removed from the area of litigation, who performs numerous and important functions in law administration that far transcend the duties of Anglo-American notaries. He is empowered by law to impart the quality of "*acte authentique*" to certain writings which must be executed before and by a public officer. He is, therefore, the official authorized to draw up and record antenuptial agreements, notarial wills, mortgages and gifts *inter vivos*. . . . As family counselor, and thus often the informal arbiter of disputes, he is, especially in smaller towns, a solidly established, eminently respectable institution. (David and de Vries, *The French Legal System*, p. 24)

Conflicting assessments of the integrity and opinions of the various notaries involved in the drawing up of Mellerio's testaments play a far greater role in this case than would be possibly appropriate if these persons were merely the equivalents of American notaries public.

As for the translation itself, although I have generally aimed at as smooth an English version as possible, I have also tried throughout to preserve traces of a French legalistic flavor. Thus, common personal titles have usually been left in the French, with "Monsieur," "Madame," and "Maître" (the title of the lawyers) romanized so they would not be too obtrusive, but with the archaic *"le sieur"* and *"la dame"* italicized to suggest their aroma of legal jargon even in the French. The names of the convent and the newspapers, as well as a few common French terms, such as street addresses, *"salon," "idée fixe,"* and so forth, have also been left untranslated, as presenting no barrier to understanding and serving as reminders of the Frenchness of the scene. To give a sense of the highly rhetorical color of the attorneys' arguments, I have conveyed as closely as possible the bias as well as the literal sense of their remarks. Where a phrase involves a play on words or some especially exotic flower of rhetoric, the original is included after the translation.

Most tense shifts have been eliminated, especially into and out of the historical present, and obvious misprints have been silently corrected. Rather than spatter the pages with footnotes, I have inserted bracketed interpolations into the text for such purposes as defining technical terms, identifying allusions, and pointing out legal stratagems and locations of counterarguments. The brackets also occasionally discuss Browning's adaptation of the point in question, but most consideration of the discrepancies between the original events and Browning's versions of them will be found in the essay in chapter five, where the poem is compared with its sources.

This study has been undertaken in the hope that the material with which it deals will serve various purposes, including the most obvious one of stimulating new interest in one of Browning's most engaging, and most neglected, long works.

It also sheds light on the particular method of transmuting inert historical data into living imaginative truth which that poem shares with its more distinguished predecessor, *The Ring and the Book*. Thus, besides revealing much about the composition of a work that certainly deserves more admiration than it has received, this study also provides an opportunity for corroborating and refining earlier studies of Browning's masterpiece. In a larger view it also contributes new material for the investigation of how various nineteenth-century writers dealt with their public's increasing reliance on the reality of objective fact and the accompanying eclipse of confidence in the value of imaginative literature. And besides, as Browning recognized, the story has a strange fascination of its own.

2

The 1872 Pleadings

[This document, and the judgment that follows in chapter four, are translations of the handwritten court records of the original trial of 1872. The pleadings consist of an identification of the various parties to the suit, the prayer for relief made by each party, and formal lists of the allegations made by the heirs and by Mme Debacker.

The plaintiffs were ten members of the Mellerio "Cousinry," as Browning calls them. (For their genealogical relation to Antonio Mellerio, see the family tree in the Appendix). The Baudry sisters were Mellerio's cousins on his mother's side. The men are listed first, as in a Shakespearean play, perhaps because in French law married women do not have independent standing before the court. Within each sex the plaintiffs are ranked according to age.

The allegations made by the heirs, which seem so conclusive here, were shown in argument to have been in fact not much more than a paraphrase of two biased documents—the one an affidavit from the family doctor, Dr. Pasquier, who had never even been to Tailleville, and the other a letter from a disreputable wandering musician named Jousse, who had been taken into the Mellerio household for a short while and then been summarily dismissed. Furthermore, the heirs never did divulge the identity of the cruel Father Joseph (numbers 41 and 50). These two interested and unsupported documents were practically the only evidence the Mellerios brought to support their case.

A second inherent weakness worth noticing in the Mellerio heirs' list of allegations is its vagueness of detail, especially where dates are concerned. In order to overturn Mellerio's testament on grounds of unsoundness of mind, it was necessary for the heirs to establish that he was insane at the exact period of his writing the testaments. To conceal the fact that they could not do that, they obscured the dating as much as possible—see especially numbers 45, 47, and 53. A major tactical revision in the allegations of the 1873 appeal was the heirs' (unsuccessful) attempt to locate the dates of their charges more precisely at the times of the drawing up of the testaments.]

SESSION OF TUESDAY, 9 JULY

1) *Le sieur* Jean François Mellerio, jeweler, residing in Paris, 9 rue de la Paix;

2) *Le sieur* Jean Antoine Mellerio, jeweler, residing in Paris, 9 rue de la Paix;

3) *Le sieur* Joseph Mellerio, jeweler, residing in Paris, 25 Quai Voltaire;

4) *Le sieur* Félix Jérôme Mellerio, residing in Paris, 6 rue d'Argenteuil;

5) *La dame* Catherine Mellerio, widow of *le sieur* Guglielmazzi, *dit* Julmasse, residing in Paris, 56 rue Caumartin;

6) *La dame* Pauline Mellerio, separated wife of *le sieur* Agnel, residing in Paris, 1 Cité Bergère, and the said *sieur* Agnel, residing in Paris;

7) *La dame* Louise Fortunée Baudry, wife of *le sieur* Julien Forcade, and this last, residing together in Paris, 11 rue Grange Batelière;

8) *La dame* Adéle Baudry, wife of *le sieur* Sureau Délinaux de Villeneuve, and this last, residing together in Arnouville (Seine et Oise);

9) *La dame* Françoise Baudry, widow of *le sieur* Beaumont, residing in Arnouville (Seine et Oise);

10) *La dame* Marie Mellerio, wife of *le sieur* Protazzi, and this last, residing together in Piedimulera, in the province of Navarre (Italy), represented by Maître Henri Lumière, attorney.

Against:

1) *La dame* Anna Sophie Trayer, separated wife of *le sieur* Achille Ferdinand Debacker, duly authorized by this last, the said *dame* residing in Tailleville and the said *sieur* Debacker residing in Paris, 18 rue de la Paix, represented by Maître Foucher, attorney.

2) *La dame* Marie Caroline Dauger, in religion Sister Saint-Remy, Mother Superior of the Convent *des Dames de la Vierge Fidèle* [Ladies of the Faithful Virgin], residing in the said Convent of la Délivrande, represented by Maître Guiomar.

Prayer for Relief

The Mellerio heirs, through Maître Henri Lumière, beg that it please the Court, while authorizing *la dame* Debacker to appear before the Court [according to French law, a married woman cannot litigate without the consent of her husband; however, if the husband's authorization cannot be obtained, the court may itself consent to allow her to plead], to declare null and void all the gifts made to *la dame* Debacker by M. Antonio Mellerio, whether *inter vivos* [between living persons] or by testaments of various dates, particularly by that of 21 October 1869; To declare equally null and void all gifts made by the said M. Antonio Mellerio to the Convent of Notre Dame de la Charité des Orphelines de Marie de la Délivrande.

Further, to authorize the plaintiffs to present testimony to establish the following facts [i.e., in a commission of inquiry]:

1) that, from the age of seventeen, M. Antonio Mellerio, having fallen prey to dissolute passions, threw himself into fashionable Parisian society, indulging in extravagant expense and scandalous misbehavior;

2) that, after having taken numerous mistresses, he eventually met in 1852 Mme Debacker, who called herself at that time Anna de Beaupré [the date given everywhere else, except for the repetition of this allegation in the list of 1873, is 1853];

3) that he was from that time on completely dominated by

27

this woman, who knew how to exert an influence over him that the passage of many years served only to increase;

4) that he openly became the lover of this woman, who succeeded in isolating him entirely, the more easily to dominate him;

5) that he never spoke of her from that time on except in such exaggerated terms as displayed the mental derangement from which he was already beginning to suffer;

6) that Mme Debacker gave him to understand that he had taken as a mistress a maiden, recently returned from England, who enjoyed a certain financial independence, whereas she was in fact married, penniless, and already the mistress of *un sieur* de Mongino;

7) that his expenses on her behalf were prodigious, and that her influence over him was such as to make him decide to leave Paris, where he had been born and had his family, his friends, and a settled way of life, to go live with her in the country, sixty leagues [150 miles] from Paris, at the château of Tailleville, where she dominated him completely;

8) that many times, nevertheless, Antonio Mellerio tried to break the chains that bound him, but he lacked the willpower necessary to persist in this resolution;

9) that in particular, during October 1867, following remonstrances made to him on this subject by his mother, he suffered a fit of madness, which lasted more than three weeks;

10) that during this *same* attack, although closely watched, he succeeded in escaping from the bedroom in which he was attended, wrapped himself in a blanket, entered the room where the servants were eating, and babbled incoherent phrases that could leave no one in any doubt about his mental condition;

11) that from that time on his mind, already weakened by the excesses of all sorts in which he had indulged, became daily still more enfeebled;

12) that in the period after the death of his mother, on 4 January 1868, the remorse he felt for his conduct induced such acts of madness and religious frenzy as astonished everyone who saw them;

13) that immediately upon arrival at his mother's resi-

dence he was forbidden by the family to reproach himself for the death of his mother, which he attributed to the sorrow he had caused her;

14) that he then swore that he would leave Mme Debacker forever and would return to a life more worthy of himself and his mother;

15) that he tried to strengthen himself in his resolution through the consolations of religion;

16) that on 8 January, the day of his mother's interment, he astonished everyone present by his strange behavior and by asking their pardon for the sorrow he had caused them;

17) that at the cemetery at Garges, his behavior was no less bizarre, and that he had to be forcibly held back from the grave where he had thrown himself, and where he said he wished to remain;

18) that his resolve to leave Mme Debacker was so fixed that he charged his friends with informing her of his decision;

19) that on 11 January the mental state of Antonio Mellerio became still more disturbing; that his speech was incoherent; that he incessantly reiterated that the specter of his past was always before him, and that he wished to atone for that past;

20) that later on that same day, Antonio Mellerio, holding a casket containing letters from Mme Debacker, plunged his hands into the fire that was burning in the grate, repeating, "Burn, burn, purify my past";

21) that, having been once snatched from the flames that were burning his hands, he succeeded in escaping, returned to the fireplace, replaced his hands in the fire, and finished burning them completely, crying always, "Burn, burn";

22) that he became violently angry with those who held him back, running about and insisting that they were preventing him from purifying himself, that the sacrifice was not yet complete;

23) that, having been put to bed, he told those present that he felt an ineffable joy at what he had done, that what he felt was celestial bliss, that his break with the past had been successful;

24) that this fit of madness lasted for some time before suf-

ficient calm could be induced to begin healing the horrible mutilation that had resulted, involving the total loss of both his hands;

25) that he continued to repeat that all relations between him and his concubine were utterly broken off, that he was going to give her a life annuity of 6,000 francs, and that he would thus have completely fulfilled his obligation to her;

26) that some days later, vague fears and fantastic terrors preyed on his mind, that he thought he saw the devil coming to pluck at his legs in the bed;

27) that Mme Debacker, who had not given up her plans for Antonio Mellerio, pursued him in her carriage whenever he went out;

28) that one day, as soon as M. Antonio Mellerio left the house of one of his relatives, he was violently seized and thrown into the carriage of Mme Debacker, who took him to her residence at 19 rue Miromesnil;

29) that on that same evening Mme Debacker could not resist saying to some friends of M. Mellerio, "Oh, if I had listened to you, I would now be wretchedly poor [*sur la paille*—lying on straw] with your miserable annuity, but now I have him";

30) that in the month of April 1868 Mme Debacker, having gained an enormous influence over the mind of Antonio Mellerio, took him back to the château of Tailleville;

31) that there a violently exaggerated religious obsession soon possessed his sick, enfeebled, and dominated mind;

32) that an almost daily communication was established between the chateau at Tailleville, the missionary priests of la Délivrande, and the Convent of la Vierge-Fidèle ["the Faithful Virgin"—the name by which the convent was known locally];

33) that, aided by the influence of Mme Debacker, the monastery and the Convent succeeded in completely dominating the mind of Antonio Mellerio, and they made whatever changes in his domestic personnel would facilitate their projects;

34) that to that end the Convent of la Délivrande was charged with, and accepted, the responsibility of finding servants for the château of Tailleville, and of making inquiries

among the inhabitants of the village of Tailleville for the purpose of hiring servants for the château;

35) that M. Mellerio had the wild idea of having mass said in a chapel he had had constructed in the château, but on the bishop's refusal to give him a chaplain he took the advice of the Superior of the Missionary Fathers of la Délivrande and requested instead that the most devout of their priests come reside at the château of Tailleville;

36) that though the estate was entailed by the testament of Mme Mellerio, his mother, he made inquiries as to how he might evade this disposition and leave his fortune to the Convent and to Mme Debacker;

37) that his religious mania increased every day, that he bought only pious books, made drawings of religious subjects, and prayed constantly;

38) that he told everyone that he was in communication with the angels, that he saw them, that they came to sustain him in the miseries of this world;

39) that he had seen them many times while going from Tailleville to la Délivrande on his knees, reciting prayers at the top of his voice;

40) that Mme Debacker said once to someone [Jousse, the wandering musician (p. 90)] with whom she was dining at the château, "I am convinced that it is only by exciting his religious ideas that I will be able to achieve my goal";

41) that she found a most wholehearted cooperation in a Father Joseph, who continually excited Antonio Mellerio's imagination by threatening him with hell and the devil;

42) that Antonio Mellerio was so terrified by these conversations that once, while playing billiards, he stopped suddenly and cried that he could see the devil in the billiard room;

43) that he would often go into ecstasies, during which times he said he was in communication with the soul of his mother, and with angels, whom he endeavored to show to people in his company;

44) that one day he removed the sacred vessels from the chapel of the château, so as not to allow them to come in contact with Mme Debacker, who he said was impure;

45) that sometimes, despite the pressure brought to bear on

31

him, there were terrible scenes of violence between Mme Debacker and M. Mellerio;

46) that he said in these moments of fury that Mme Debacker was not fit to eat at the same table with respectable people;

47) that there were often at night dreadful scenes, during which Antonio Mellerio was heard to utter pitiful cries;

48) that Mme Debacker went about always armed, causing real terror among the inhabitants of the château;

49) that, to make her domination more complete, Mme Debacker succeeded in driving away all the former servants of the château;

50) that Antonio said many times that he had given money to the church because the devil terrified him, and that Father Joseph was very cruel to him;

51) that one day, being alone with someone [Jousse], he said, "The only way for me to escape the situation I am in is to marry. You have a daughter—I ask your permission to marry her."

52) that the terror Mme Debacker inspired and the indignation that her conduct aroused made several servants leave the château of Tailleville;

53) that Mme Debacker dismissed other servants because they took the liberty of coming to the defense of their master;

54) that during the month of October 1869 he frequently bathed in a large tub of water that he called his bath of purification, and in which he also wished to have the servants immersed [for the marvellously bizarre details concerning this bath of purification, see the 1873 list of allegations in chapter 6, nos. 74–84];

55) that he insistently urged one young servant in his employ to take off all his clothes and kneel in a state of nudity, to imitate, he said, the angels and the cherubim in their adoration of our Lord Jesus Christ;

56) that on another day of the same year, he dug a hole in the château park where he buried the meat that had been intended for dinner, because he claimed one should not eat meat that day;

57) that a few hours later he left for Courseulles, where he ordered dinner, with meat;

58) that all his behavior revealed a complete deterioration of his rational faculties, that everyone who dealt with him observed this condition, that one person who saw him frequently said, in the last months of 1869, "Antonio is madder than ever—never again will he be able to undertake anything serious";

59) that at that time he often challenged his neighbors to duels over quarrels about rabbit-hunting, and every day he performed acts that unmistakably revealed his unsoundness of mind;

60) that on 13 April 1870 M. Mellerio, who had just left Mme Debacker, hurriedly climbed the stairs of the château and threw himself from the top of his belvedere to the ground, dying instantly;

61) that on that very day a doctor who had often seen him said, "It was to be expected—we knew it would happen eventually";

62) that many times before he had stated his intention to commit suicide;

63) that it was common knowledge in the region that Antonio Mellerio no longer had the free exercise of his will, that he was completely dominated by Mme Debacker, and that everyone knew that his various testaments and gifts were nothing more than the joint result of undue influence and unsoundness of mind.

To appoint a Commissioner [*Juge Commissaire*] to chair a commission of inquiry; to charge the costs incurred in this case against the defendants; and to order execution of the provisional remedy contained in the judgment of 4 March 1872. [The executor of the testament would have asked the court for a provisional remedy, to settle these issues, in order not to have to decide for himself and perhaps be sued for conversion in case he guessed wrong. Filing such a request would have barred Mme Debacker from selling anything in the estate or even from deriving any income from it—hence her request in the next paragraph for an allowance for interim expenses.] To declare and adjudge that Mme Debacker be required within one week of judgment to yield possession and enjoyment of the château of Tailleville, which she has continued without legal right to occupy since the death of M.

Mellerio. To order the execution of this judgment, opposition or appeal notwithstanding and without bond. [One possible action for the court to take would be to give the heirs the estate, but also to require them to post a bond to cover any loss of the estate's value in case a successful appeal was later brought against them. Not requiring a bond would imply that in the court's opinion an appeal would be unlikely to succeed.] To deny the petition made by Mme Debacker to receive temporary support from the assets of the estate. Signed: Henri Lumière.

Mme Debacker begs, through Maître Foucher, attorney, that it please the Court, in considering jointly the suit brought by Mme Debacker for a writ of possession together with the suit brought by the Mellerio heirs for nullification of gifts and testaments, while authorizing Mme Debacker to appear before this Court: to disregard the petition for a commission of inquiry, which should be rejected as unnecessary, inadmissible, inconclusive, and illegitimate; to deny totally and entirely the claims of MM. Jean Mellerio and others; to allow Mme Debacker to take possession of the legacy in her favor contained in the testament of 21 October 1869, and if necessary [i.e., in case this testament is not upheld] deliver to her the gifts contained in those of 27 June 1869, 4 June 1868, and 25 February 1865; to rule that in any case a sum of 1,000 francs per month be paid to Mme Debacker for interim expenses, beginning from 13 April 1870, the date of the death of M. Mellerio; to order the provisionary execution of this judgment, appeal notwithstanding, and without payment of bond. With costs.

Further, in the remote case that the commission of inquiry might conceivably be ordered, to authorize Mme Debacker to submit evidence in refutation; further, to authorize her to present testimony to establish the following facts:

1) that in 1855 and 1856 Antonio Mellerio's parents came to Tailleville to spend two summers in succession with M. Mellerio and Mme Debacker, that they lived together and took their meals together, that Mme Mellerio declared repeatedly to friends that she would be happy to have her son marry Mme Debacker if she were free;

2) that the first message sent to M. Antonio Mellerio [at

Tailleville on the occasion of his mother's death in Paris] did not arrive until the evening of 4 January 1868, that this message only spoke of an indisposition, that M. Mellerio left for Paris the morning of the fifth, that only on the evening of the fifth did a second message arrive announcing the death of Mme Mellerio, that Mme Debacker herself then left for Paris on the morning of the sixth;

3) that in 1868, during the months of February and March, the cousins of M. Mellerio themselves recognized that he enjoyed the full play of his mental faculties, and after a family council they agreed that he should continue the management of his own affairs;

4) that in the years 1868 and 1869 M. Mellerio often repeated to friends that it was his fixed resolve to leave his estate to Mme Debacker, that after his last testament he continued to use the same language, adding that after the death of Mme Debacker the property of Tailleville should belong to the orphanage to which he had made charitable donations during his lifetime;

5) that during the years 1868, 1869, and 1870 M. Mellerio had often declared to these same friends that it was his fixed resolve never to leave his estate to his cousins. To charge the costs of the case against the plaintiffs, to reject the action for removal brought against Mme Debacker. Signed: A. Foucher.

The Convent of Notre Dame de la Charité des Orphelines de Marie de la Délivrande, through Maître Guiomar, attorney, begs that it please the Court to dismiss the suit brought by MM. Mellerio and others as not stating a claim upon which relief can be founded, with costs to be refunded to the undersigned attorney, who hereby certifies having advanced them. Signed. Maître Guiomar.

Issues:

1) Should the Court, in considering jointly the suit brought by Mme Debacker for a writ of replevin [recovery of goods detained until court action], together with the suit for a nullification of dispositions made to her, while authorizing her to appear before this Court, immediately declare reasonable or inadmissible the petition of nullification of the said dispositions as well as those made to the Convent of

Notre Dame de la Charité des Orphelines de Marie de la Délivrande, or, before deciding this point, should it permit the
said Mellerio heirs to submit evidence supporting the allegations listed by them?

2) Should the Court, if the commission of inquiry be ordered, grant a temporary order requiring *la dame* Debacker
to yield possession and enjoyment of the château of Tailleville?

3) Should the Court, in any case, grant *la dame* Debacker
the interim expenses requested by her?

4) Who should pay costs?

3

The 1872 Trial

[This extensive account of the trial is taken from *L'Ordre et la Liberté*, for reasons explained in the Introduction. Portions of other newspapers, for comparison or amplification, are occasionally included in brackets. The story ran from 19 June to 10 July 1872, and covered the three days of the lawyers' arguments and rebuttals (17-19 June), the public prosecutor's summary (3 July), and the court's announcement of its judgment (8 July).]

[*L'Ordre et la Liberté*, Wednesday, 19 June 1872]

Judicial Chronicle
Civil Court of Caen
First Chamber

President: M. *le président* Pellerin
Prosecuting Magistrate: M. Cosnard-Desclozets, Public Prosecutor [*procureur de la République*]

The Mellerio heirs against:

1) *la dame* Sophie Trayer, separated wife of M. Debacker, residing at Paris;

2) and this latter to authorize her;

3) and the Convent of Notre Dame de la Charité des Orphelines de Marie de la Délivrande.

Session of 17 June 1872

The session begins at 11:00. Among the distinguished visitors are General de Vendeuvre, the public prosecutor [*le procureur général*], and several magistrates of this and the lower Court. The bar [the space reserved for the participants] is completely full, with a large crowd squeezed into the section set aside for the public. Ladies throng the courtroom. The President of the Court has thoughtfully provided convenient space for the press, a kind attention for which we would like to take this opportunity to express our appreciation.

At the beginning of the session, several other matters are taken up and quickly disposed of. Finally comes the case whose title we have given above.

Maître Allou, of the Paris bar, whose reputation is of the very highest order, represents the plaintiffs. Maître Pilet des Jardins; [*pilet* is French for "pin-tailed duck"] of the same bar, whose excellent administration as subprefect the district of Bayeux still remembers, is charged with defending the interests of Mme Debacker. Maître Carel, our own eminent and popular professor of law, represents the Convent of la Délivrande.

The pleadings are read. The husband of Mme Debacker is dismissed.

Maître Allou has the floor.

(We make no pretense of being able adequately to render in print a rhetoric at once so sober and so spirited, an oratory kept so effortlessly at the highest level of verbal art, and filled with enlightening observations whenever appropriate, a tone of integrity in which are expressed inferences intertwined and flowing as if from a spring—in short, an eloquence that attracts by its charm and seeks to convince without fatiguing. We can give only an imperfect paraphrase.)

I wish, says Maître Allou, to retrace the facts for you with all the faithfulness of an eyewitness. Certainly this claim may sound dubious, coming as it does from the counsel for the plaintiffs, but I assure you that I will indeed do so, and with all possible moderation.

The *de cuius* [the person "on whose account" the suit is brought], Antonio Mellerio, was born in 1827. His father, of Italian origin, was one of the most illustrious and respected [*les plus considérables et les plus considérés*] jewelers of Paris.

Two sons were born to the Mellerios, one dying before them, the other—Antonio—surviving them. [For details see the family history, chapter 6.] Handsome, generous, tender to those who loved him in spite of the sorrows his excesses caused them, full of high spirits and imagination, a lover of the arts, but also extremely impressionable, overwrought, a slave of the passion of the moment, violent, incapable of moderation—as one of his friends put it, leaping from the first to the sixth floor at a single bound—and with all this, as is so often the case with such exuberant natures, all too easily influenced—such was Antonio, as he threw himself as a youth into the midst of the dissipations of Parisian society.

Maître Allou cites from Antonio's letters various passages that reveal the violence of Antonio's character as well as his love of luxury. He had innumerable mistresses. It is vain to claim in his defense that he sometimes wrote to his younger brother in the role of sage, since his actual conduct was not at all that of a Mentor [Ulysses' counselor, Telemachus' tutor], and these very letters testify to the contradictoriness of his nature.

Then follows a reading from the letters of some passages so licentiously erotic that they necessarily lead to a very pronounced movement of fans among the ladies present in the room. It will be understood that none of this reading can be transcribed here. Such matters are not, observes Maître Allou, the simple follies one finds on lifting a corner of the curtain concealing the youth of even the most respectable men; this is a desolating display of dissipation and debauchery [un désolant tableau de dissipation et de débauche]. These are not yet the disorders of a deranged mind, but they are disorders indicating a mind that is not entirely master of its passions. And the exigencies of the case do not permit that they remain concealed.

Under such circumstances Antonio met Mme Debacker. Various documents, belonging not to this lady but to the Mellerio estate and deposited with Maître Prevost, a family lawyer in Paris, have been legitimately given by him to the heirs, and they throw some light on this intrigue.

Sophie Trayer was born in Metz, in 1830. Her father was a brigadier in the national guard. In 1849 she married in Paris a struggling tailor, M. Debacker. The Debacker couple went to live in London, where Fortune did not smile on them any more than she had in Paris. In 1852 Sophie Trayer returned alone to live with her mother. She later maintained that she had fled her husband because he would have exploited her beauty. She was first kept by a M. de Mongino. [This allegation about M. de Mongino was vigorously, and unsupportedly, denied (p. 66).] She called herself Anna de Beaupré. [The "de," of course, constituted a fraudulent claim to aristocratic background. For a fuller comment on this name and the implications of Browning's replacement of it by "Clara de Millefleurs," see this author's study in *ELH* (11 [June 1974]: 283–87).] In January 1853 Antonio met the mother and daughter at the theater. He introduced himself to them; he became the lover of Mme Debacker, whom at first he thought to have been unmarried. We cannot reproduce the letters to his brother in which he announces this *good* fortune, for the same reasons that applied above.

The story that Anna de Beaupré gave Mellerio was that she had been pursued to London, where she had meant to become an actress, by two eminent personages, the Prince d'O . . . , and Lord N . . . ; the latter wished to marry her. The prince had departed, she spurned the lord, and in return Antonio burned the letters of his own previous paramours.

They took up residence in the rue Miromesnil.

At first contenting himself with merely accepting some gifts from Mellerio, Anna soon involved him in enormous expenses, even including the payment of her old debts.

M. Debacker reappeared on the scene, having returned to Paris, and having soon thereafter become a celebrated tailor under the name of "Alfred." He had bought a property in Paris for more than 500,000 francs, in the name of a Mlle Viel, but reserved a life estate therein for himself. "This building was later burned by the deplorable violence [*les outrages*] of the Commune, but what is left is restorable." [The reporter was here presumably quoting Maître Allou verbatim. I cannot guess why.] He desired to break legally with his wife; he surprised the household in the rue Miromesnil, and filed charges of adultery against the two lovers, but ultimately settled for a judicial separation. [In the appeal it was made clear that M. Debacker, now allied with this Mlle Viel, intended by these maneuvers to prevent Mme Debacker from claiming her share of her husband's new wealth.]

Antonio's father had bought, in Calvados, the estate of Tailleville, and enjoyed residing there occasionally with his wife. In their absence Antonio installed his mistress in residence. The defense implies that there was a sort of tacit consent to this arrangement. The plaintiffs reject this interpretation. Antonio and Mme Debacker left very soon after the arrival of the parents. If Mme Mellerio ever tolerated finding Anna at the bedside of her sick son, and should even have concealed her indignation in order to thank her for her care, that is understandable. But never did this mother, this respectable and honorable woman, accept a communal life under such sordid conditions, in association with such a couple.

Above all, never did she praise such a situation, never did she let it be understood that she wished marriage could have legitimized it. For the mistress who had stolen Antonio from his family, his profession, and a respectable life, this mother had nothing but curses.

Antonio's father died [in 1860]. The settlement gave his son at least 300,000 francs, free and clear.

Antonio asked his mother's permission to restore Tailleville, to accomplish which project he indulged in outlandish expense.

In October 1867, in Paris, he took a cold bath. Having thereby caught a fever, he took to his bed, and suddenly one day wrapped himself in a blanket and descended like a ghost to the jewelry shop, where he ranted wildly. Thus appeared the first symptoms of that unsoundness of mind (*insanité d'esprit*) of which the last stage would be suicide. [This was the first appearance of the plaintiffs' insistent efforts to link Mellerio's death to his history of eccentricity. The defendants would counter, and the court agree, that an interpretation of suicide is at least improbable and is certainly irrelevant to his state of mind when drawing up his testament six months earlier (pp. 61, 78, 102, and 118).]

In November, Antonio returned to Tailleville.

Shortly afterward, on the evening of 4 January 1868, in Paris, Mme Mellerio had a sudden fit of acute apoplexy and died. On the same evening, or on the morning of the fifth, M. Morel, a friend of the family and its faithful financial agent, sent Antonio a message to prepare him for this cruel news. Antonio arrived in Paris on January sixth, thinking to find his mother ill. The plaintiffs are reproached with not having intercepted him in order to warn him, and with having thus struck such an impressionable mind so cruel a blow. But they did not know on which day or by what train he would be arriving.

Upon entering the house, he learned of the fatal event. It is understandable that grief and remorse for the pains he had caused his mother would seize him violently, considering his extremely intense nature, and that the desire for reparation would plunge him for the time being into an overwrought state of agitation. The family had piously awaited his arrival before proceeding with the interment; he did not dare enter the death chamber, he declared himself unworthy, he confessed his faults, he begged forgiveness from everyone. Maître Allou does not pry here for traces of madness. He respects this expression of intense emotion flowing from an excess of both sorrow and remorse.

Antonio, at the urging of a priest and two nuns, finally brought himself to kiss his mother's remains. Swearing to break with the past, he entered her room, and calmly stood by the bureau. By a testament dated at the top 6 January and at the bottom 7 January—a confusion that is easily attributed to the distress into which he was thrown by his mother's death—he bequeathed his entire estate to his natural heirs, excepting only 150,000 francs for Mme Debacker, with whom he wished to break off all relations.

Alone, independently, he made these arrangements, and his youth [Mellerio was 41] could not lead the family to expect to profit by them. There was no opportunity for them to interfere. Morel was Antonio's only adviser, and was made the guardian of this document.

Afterward, Antonio asked for a priest, and called in his friends. His frenzy returned, the violent behavior of his arrival reappeared, and then suddenly his attention turned to trivial details and distractions.

On the day of the interment, Antonio publicly repeated his pleas for forgiveness. At the cemetery of Garges, where the ceremony of burial took place, he threw himself into the grave. What incredible agony! What incredible impulsiveness!

Upon his return whom did he find on the stairway? Mme Debacker. He told her that all was over between them, that his mother had wished it to be so. He sent friends to her to negotiate a break and to determine the amount of an annuity for her. His friends and Morel persuaded him to take his rightful place as head of the household, and to start a new and wholesome life. He seemed firmly committed to these resolutions.

On 11 January he dined with Morel; he kissed him and called him his savior. Morel left him for a moment, and on his return a horrible spectacle met his eyes—Antonio crouching before the hearth, holding in the flames of the fireplace a crystal casket containing Mme Debacker's letters. The fire burned his hands and shattered the crystal, but he seemed to feel nothing as he rocked back and forth, chanting in a strange rhythm, "Burn! burn! purify my past!"

Morel snatched him from this torture. Antonio, being stronger, freed himself and returned to his appalling ritual. Again Morel snatched him away, dragging and rolling him over the floor. Antonio heaped reproaches on him, cursing him for preventing the completion of his purification. He was completely obsessed with his past, with his mother, and with the frenzy that he called his reparation.

He lost all his fingers and parts of his hands. It was with great difficulty that he was kept alive at all. The cure was accomplished by the brilliant expertise of his devoted doctor, Dr. Pasquier, a medical officer later foully murdered at the Pont de Neuilly by the Communards [members of the Commune of Paris, in 1871], to whom he had been sent with a flag of truce. [This high praise of Dr. Pasquier was in preparation for the later introduction of his crucial, and much disputed, affidavit—pp. 48, 63–64. For the public prosecutor's full consideration of this document, see p. 104. In the judgment itself the court remarked that "in order to prove Antonio Mellerio's unsoundness of mind, the plaintiffs rely primarily on the affidavit of Dr. Pasquier" (pp. 117–18).

There is no mention of this aspect of the case in Browning's poem.]

Antonio survived with two shapeless stumps, which were later fitted up with special attachments so that he could make attempts to write or to draw, when he did not perform these activities with his mouth. There are several specimens of his work in the dossier submitted to the Court. [Mellerio's ability to write with his mouth was to be a significant element in the family's loss of their first appeal, which was largely based on the claim that the last testament must have been a forgery because it was not in Mellerio's handwriting. The defense successfully countered this claim by reminding the court of Mellerio's facility with his mouth, and by pointing out that in any case the family could not really be serious about the charges of forgery because they had not even mentioned it in the original suit.]

But what became of his reason in the course of this episode? It foundered completely. The fit of frenzy completely destroyed his mind.

In various letters written to M. Hébert, a notary at Douvres, M. Morel discussed Antonio's illness, though in extremely discreet terms. The defendants rely heavily on these letters to establish that this devoted friend of the family did not consider Antonio's mind to be at all deranged. But such acknowledgments are never made by relatives or intimate friends! The letters deal with such matters as an improvement of his mental condition, a formal consultation of the assembled family, Antonio's continuing to manage his business affairs, and medical advice against his being legally declared incompetent.

This was not Antonio's first experience at breaking off a sentimental relationship. During his mother's lifetime he had lost his heart to a young girl who was poor but honest [honnête, mais pauvre]. He asked Mme Mellerio's permission to marry her. Happy to see him give up his liaison with Anna, Mme Mellerio agreed, on condition that the girl was respectable. He installed her at Quai Voltaire [his mother's house], with due regard to all the proprieties. But his reserve was short-lived—his fiancée became a mother. The dream was soon over.

It is always possible, says Mme de Sevigné, to find an honorable way to end a dishonorable affair. It was just such a way Antonio wished to find with Mme Debacker. It was in vain that Morel told her that Antonio had left for Italy. She discovered the truth, she spied on him, she followed him in the parks, in the city, everywhere. Finally, one day, when he was leaving a relative's house, she threw herself into his carriage; she seized him, slammed the door, and flung the coachman the address: 19 rue Miromesnil.

That evening he returned to Quai Voltaire and related his adventure to Morel, telling him that he had that day found not a mistress but a sister. He led his friend to Mme Debacker. "If I had listened to you," said she to Morel, "I would now be wretchedly poor with your miserable annuity, but now I have him!" ["*Je le tiens!*" This dramatic version of Mme Debacker's kidnapping Mellerio was flatly denied by the defense, whose own version of the lovers' reunion was supported not only by a compliment to her in a letter from Morel a few days later (pp. 65–66) but even by the account of the episode given in Dr. Pasquier's affidavit (p. 64).]

He left Quai Voltaire for the rue Miromesnil, and soon they left Paris for Tailleville; and thus their life together began again.

Financially, Antonio found himself very well off: after the deduction of all expenses, even the money lavished on the remodeling of Tailleville, Mme Mellerio's estate amounted to 1,500,000 francs. Including the wealth he had inherited from his father, Antonio found that he had an income of 60,000 francs a year.

The Court was adjourned from one to two o'clock.

At the opening of the afternoon session, Maître Allou continues.

At Tailleville, Mme Debacker reawoke Antonio's old passion. She held him, weakened by the debauchery of the past and the violent shocks he had recently experienced; she held him, mutilated and defenseless. He was in her power. She tyrannized over him, interfered with his correspondence, and left him uncared for and badly clothed.

The defendants have sought to give the impression that regular social relations were established within the community of Tailleville. But such was not the case at all. Artistic and literary types may have been gathered from nearby beach resorts, but no significant contact occurred with any respectable persons in the region.

Mellerio underwent a transformation. Given his impressionable, unsteady, and immoderate nature, his dreadful experiences caused him complete mental deterioration.

He fell prey to a spirit of mysticism. He had strange visions, and in front of his servants he indulged in the most bizarre eccentricities. Nowadays particularly [only one year after the Commune], when so much of our social structure is weakened, the speaker has no need to dwell on how necessary it is to respect the institutions of society. But this kind of behavior was not religion—this was eccentricity, this was insanity.

Profaning so honorable a cause as religion, Mme Debacker exploited Antonio's condition under the veil of hypocrisy. [Apparently hoping to win the case without displaying the most embarrassing of their cousin's behavior, the plaintiffs did not go here into sordid detail. In the 1873 list of allegations, more desperate to win the appeal, they were less discreet.]

To this end she relied on works of charity, becoming involved with the two religious establishments of la Délivrande. [Besides the convent, there is a monastery of missionary priests associated with the church of la Délivrande, but it did not figure largely in the case.] These involvements delighted Mellerio, who found himself often associated with good works, and he eventually even asked for a personal chaplain. But the Church refused him this favor as long as Mme Debacker remained at Tailleville.

We come to the end of the drama.

In April 1870 the carriage was prepared; instead of entering it, he climbed up to a belvedere that his poor mother, as if warned by a fatal presentiment, had regretted to see built; he leaped to join the angels, fell, and died. [This concise sentence contains the climax of Browning's poem, in which version Mellerio pauses on the brink to deliver a 303-line soliloquy.]

The defendants maintain that in intending to water the

plants around the balustrade he became dizzy, and that his fall was a completely involuntary accident. But it was not Mellerio's task to water the plants, and besides, the extreme height of the balustrade and the absence of his hands both forbade it.

Some souls are hardy spirits, who seek repose in a voluntary death, killing themselves in full possession of their reason. Such is the strength of a man who can at will either live or destroy himself. Such is the doctrine of the Stoics. Certainly it is erroneous, because it is our sacred duty to stay at our posts to the end, to fight the battle of life. But at any rate, such a death is not the act of a weakened mind.

But here, on the contrary, at the end of Mellerio's existence, when he threw himself into space to rejoin his mother and the angels, ah! there we find the act of a will no longer master of itself—there is an act of pure madness.

Public opinion was not deceived. A newspaper of the region published a story giving this account of the event. The gardener, or rather Mme Debacker through the gardener, was the only person to protest it. [This account appeared in the *Bonhomme Normand*, 23–29 April 1870: "Last week, M. Mellerio, proprietor of the château of Tailleville, near St. Aubin-sur-Mer, ended his days by throwing himself from the belvedere on the roof of his château.

"The estate of Tailleville is known as one of the most beautiful in the region, as much for its location, one-and-a-half kilometers from the sea, as for the tastefulness with which it is laid out: farm, impressive living quarters, chapel, parks, gardens, woods, magnificent hunting preserves— nothing is lacking, including a fine art gallery containing examples of the works of the great masters.

"But in spite of his immense fortune, M. Mellerio was not happy, since fate had thrown in his path a woman who had gained total control over his weakened mental condition. Indeed, on one occasion, convinced that he faced damnation because of his illicit relations with her, he placed both hands in the fire and burned off all his fingers, leaving only shapeless stumps that were thereafter always covered with leather gloves tipped with wood.

"In recent days, the master of Tailleville, a warmhearted

and charitable man, devoted much of his attention to nearby churches and convents, to which he is reported to have left a significant portion of his estate.

"M. Mellerio was forty-three."]

[This account is the one that Mme Debacker's outraged counsel would later claim had been deliberately planted by the Mellerios for exactly this purpose—to be used as "evidence" that the whole region "knew" that Mellerio was being unduly influenced.]

On receiving the news of his death, Dr. Pasquier, then still alive, gave an opinion that clearly characterized the leap as an act of madness.

Antonio had made several testaments. [The following paragraphs are a clear (and uncontested) summary of the chronology of the five testaments and the annuity. For another, see pp. 97–98.] In 1865 he left 120,000 francs to Mme Debacker, appointing M. Hébert, notary at Douvres, executor of his testament. At the death of his mother [January 1868], he increased this legacy to 150,000 francs and left the residue of his estate to his cousins.

On 4 June 1868 he left half his estate to Mme Debacker. In September 1868 he gave her an annual income of 12,000 francs, beginning from that very day. In June 1869 he added (a rather peculiar phrase, because it in fact destroyed the previous arrangements) a clause making the said lady his sole beneficiary, and stipulating that after her death Tailleville was to be converted into an asylum or hospital for the maimed poor, to be called St. Joseph's. The park was to be maintained by M. Legendre or his descendants, or by M. Richer, the head gardener. This last provision is certainly eccentric.

Finally, on 21 October 1869, in a testament undoubtedly drawn up by a professional, he made Mme Debacker his sole beneficiary, except for 1) Tailleville and its outbuildings, and 2) a sum of 200,000 francs, all of which, after the death of his legatee, was to go to the Convent of la Charité des Orphelines de la Délivrande.

Maître Allou submits that on the part of Mme Debacker there was undue influence. He asks what has become of 300,000 francs missing from Antonio's estate, and what is the meaning of some large bills he has been shown, which were not inventoried in the estate and were described there as "wastepaper." [For the defendants' response to the charges of the missing 300,000 francs and the "wastepaper," see p. 62.]

With regard to the various testaments, he poses the question of unsoundness of mind. Certainly Mellerio's cousins dealt with him in various financial affairs, notably in their purchase of the jewelry business and its stock-in-trade. But Mellerio could have been completely in possession of his faculties at the time of such acts and yet no longer have been of sound mind when Mme Debacker, using her influence over him, had the last testament drawn up, with her role in its creation veiled by a pious donation. [This passage represents the plaintiffs' attempt to answer one of the defendants' most unanswerable arguments—that as men of integrity the family would certainly not have negotiated such complex (and favorable) financial arrangements with a man they even suspected of being mentally unbalanced.]

Likewise, Mellerio's cousins could find themselves under the same roof as Mme Debacker, and politely endure her presence without thereby ever being reconciled to it or ever approving of the purported rehabilitation *à deux* in which she was involved with Antonio at Tailleville.

The heirs made an attempt at settlement. In the draft thereof, signed by Mme Debacker, she acknowledged some acts of eccentricity on Antonio's part. She was offered a life estate in Tailleville plus an annuity of 12,000 francs. She demanded 15,000 francs; her request was denied. Then Mme Debacker's counsel in Paris demanded on her behalf an annuity of 18,000 francs. The heirs finally consented. But then reappeared the opulent tailor, the husband, M. Debacker, otherwise known as "Alfred," the man of fashion, who emerged from his fitting-room and refused to give his authorization to an annuity of less than 25,000 francs. Faced with these outrageous demands, the attempt at compromise was broken off. The subject was never broached with the Convent. [This episode certainly suggests that Mme Debacker was aware of at least some merit in the legal issues raised by the family. The whole question of her acquiescence in various settlement schemes is omitted in Browning's version, where she is shown as indignantly spurning all such suggestions. For a full discussion of this point, see pp. 142–43.]

The Convent, for its part, is seen to be conducting itself with extreme prudence, "and if the case is decided in favor of the heirs, it no doubt reserves the right to retire with dignity behind the folds of its immaculate robe." (Laughter.) [The innuendo concerns the new dogma of Immaculate Conception.]

Maître Allou declares that it is with regret that he sees that his remarks could be interpreted as containing any unpleasant allusion. He respects both religion and the Court too much to indulge in tasteless humor.

Perhaps it might be said that the Convent was insufficiently circumspect in becoming involved with the illegitimate *ménage* at Tailleville, but there was no shameless [*éhontée*] undue influence on the part of the Convent of la Délivrande. The heirs seek the annulment of all gifts made to the detriment of the family.

On account of the grave implications revealed by the facts, both those concerning undue influence as well as those concerning the unsoundness of mind of the *de cuius*, the family ask for a commission of inquiry, for which they specify the points to be examined.

They agree to a provision of 1,000 francs per month for Mme Debacker, but they also ask that in order not to influence the commission she leave Tailleville and take up residence in the rue Miromesnil.

The session will be continued tomorrow.

[*L'Ordre et la Liberté*, Thursday, 20 June 1872]

Session of 18 June 1872

The President gives the floor to Maître Pilet des Jardins, counsel for Mme Debacker.

We will summarize as before.

The Mellerio family are contesting Antonio's testamentary dispositions, by charging both undue influence and unsoundness of mind. "I come," says Maître Pilet des Jardins, "to defend the last wishes of a man with whom I was personally acquainted. I must struggle against the talents of an opponent who is one of our most distinguished attorneys, and to perform this duty at all I must first overcome my sense of inadequacy.

"My adversary began by saying that he would speak like an eyewitness. As for myself, I will begin by declaring that I myself do not wish to be a witness, that I do not desire any personal point of view at all. The facts will speak for themselves; the facts will be their own witnesses.

"Thus it will be the correspondence between Antonio and his brother that will bring to light Antonio's character. I do not mean that this will be done by facts cleverly chosen for the exigencies of the case, as was done by our opponents, but by the correspondence exactly as it is, exactly as it paints him."

The speaker then raises the question of unsoundness of mind. It has been claimed that Antonio escaped the clutches of erotic mania only then to fall prey to religious mania. Maître Allou's portrait of this young man is drawn from the biased account provided for him by his clients, and not from the wholesome expressions of common sense contained in the correspondence. Although he has admittedly perceived certain *noble* qualities in Antonio, he has spared no pains to portray him as unsteady, violent, easily influenced, and so forth.

According to Mme Debacker's counsel, a reading of the correspondence in no way supports this opinion.

Of Italian origin, M. Mellerio senior, whose integrity and high commercial standing are matters of public knowledge, was a real artist. Like him, his two sons were also artistic; like him, they also were endowed with a generous nature. Mme Mellerio, as fine a wife as she was a mother, raised her children as Christians, in every sense of the word. [For Joseph Mellerio's allegations to the contrary, see the family history, chapter 6.] Thus, when Antonio had the sorrow of losing her, is it surprising to see him return to the religious sentiments that, even in the midst of his youthful errors, he had never entirely abandoned?

It has been alleged that his behavior toward his mother

was violent. In support of this allegation, only one single event has been cited, which if it really happened would be most regrettable but which would nevertheless remain isolated. And even of that event where is the proof? [It is not clear what this event might have been.]

This tall, strong, and athletic youth, as has been remarked, became a "little girl"—it is his own expression—"in the presence of his parents." In his affectionate letters to his brother Victor, from which the lawyer reads passages, he speaks equally as fondly of his parents. This brother, some years younger than he and often mistaken for him, was a spendthrift; Antonio redoubled his wise advice, and if he often seems to accuse himself, offering himself as a bad example, it is only for the purpose of bringing his lesson home more forcibly. He said so himself.

Because he confesses, *with regret*, having lost some louis, at Roger's and on one or two other occasions, he is taxed with having been a gambler. Because he jokes, "I get tipsy [*je me grise*] every Saturday at Roger's," the remark is taken literally and he is considered a drunkard, as if the style of Roger's hospitality permitted supposing any such thing! [This "Roger" was an eminent operatic singer to whom Mellerio later sent a portrait drawn with his mutilated hands—pp. 74 and 124.]

His entire correspondence, and it is all there in the record, establishes that he never forgot his affection for his family, and that even in the midst of his pleasure he was often occupied with business responsibilities.

(See particularly a letter of February 1853, at which time, it should be remembered, he was already involved with Mme Debacker.)

His letters are full of verve and youthful exuberance. They are not the work of a man helpless in the grip of passion.

After a series of amorous exploits [*des incartades*] that were entirely appropriate to the elegant Parisian society in which he mixed, and that do not deserve in his case any more than in that of others to be characterized as erotic mania, he met Mme Debacker. The plaintiffs have already, in their denunciatory vein, told the story of this relationship, through documents obtained from the family attorney, Maître Prevost. It is not necessary to retrace this incident, which may be judged as soon as it has been heard and which has at any rate already been dwelt on at great length.

Maître Pilet des Jardins does not wish to defend the propriety of Mme Debacker's past history. In that history, which has been incredibly exaggerated by the plaintiffs, there may be seen to be highly extenuating circumstances, when viewed in the proper perspective. But the attorney refuses to bring either her husband or her mother into the picture. The term "courtesan" [*une femme galante*] has been used; it is a gross exaggeration. Mme Debacker remained faithful to Antonio from the day she met him, and she brought him a tranquility that he had never known before.

As far as morality and the laws of society are concerned, she is no doubt at fault for her participation in this irregular situation. But as far as Antonio was concerned—and this is the most important point of the entire lawsuit—she is irreproachable. Friends, advisers, the heirs themselves—all heaped compliments on her, right up to the day of Antonio's death; on two occasions she even resided at Tailleville with M. and Mme Mellerio, where the latter accorded her signs of sympathy that are recorded in written evidence and that cannot be denied.

In 1857 Antonio suffered the loss of his brother, whom he loved dearly. In 1860 the death of his father struck yet another blow to his affections. The more the ranks thinned, the closer he drew to Mme Debacker; the more the void opened around him, the more this youth [in 1860 Antonio was 33] who was all heart [*qui était tout coeur*] tried to fill it by increasing their mutual affection.

M. Debacker, whose personal morality is not at issue here, decided that he ought to have his wife's behavior investigated. He later brought a criminal complaint against her, but withdrew it at a price: her renunciation of her right to their common property. She consented. Now, there were more than 100,000 francs involved in this sacrifice, because M. Debacker was already in the full flush of prosperity. But Mme Debacker chose to stay with Antonio, whose father, mother, and brother were at that time all still alive. It certainly cannot have been greed that guided her.

53

At the death of his father, the terms of the settlement fell far short of giving Antonio the 300,000 francs that the heirs have alleged.

Antonio's artistic tastes led him to embellish Tailleville; the prodigalities attributed to him have no basis in fact. Letters submitted to the Court show that Mme Mellerio approved both the plans and the expense; on one occasion she even reproached Antonio for the apparent diffidence with which he asked her for money!

The mad scene of October 1867, after the cold bath (in the so-called "erotic period"), sustains close examination no better than these other allegations do. Dr. Pasquier, the friend of the family, actually advised convalescence at Tailleville, where Mme Debacker was residing. A strange remedy for erotic mania! [For the plaintiffs' rebuttal, see p. 83.]

But what is most important is to watch Antonio's desire to assure that the financial security of Mme Debacker begin and grow, stage by stage, with careful thought, under many varied circumstances. [This was a cornerstone of the defendants' case: the steady increment of Mme Debacker's share in Mellerio's various testaments must have implied a correspondingly steady increment in his regard for her, whatever may have been his occasional lapses into "eccentricity." The heirs would counter that, on the contrary, the sequence of testaments merely displayed the progressive success of Mme Debacker's campaign of undue influence—p. 90. In its judgment the court would point out that in fact, since the 1865 bequest occurred before any eccentricity was even alleged, the only real issue in the case could be the amount Mme Debacker should receive, not at all whether she should be left out entirely—p. 119.]

In 1865, after thirteen years of intimacy, while his mother was still alive, he bequeathed to Mme Debacker 120,000 francs. He had not yet had any of those attacks of which the Court has heard. His intention is already clearly manifest. He left her more than one-third of his total estate at that time.

In 1868, on Saturday, 4 January, Mme Mellerio suddenly died. Antonio was first sent a message that merely mentioned an indisposition. Tailleville does not even have a telegraph office, so Antonio did not receive the message until midnight. On Sunday morning he departed for Paris alone. That evening a second message arrived at Tailleville announcing the whole unhappy truth. But Antonio was en route. He arrived in Paris at about six o'clock, with no one to meet him and no one to warn him. His reaction has already been described, and it is not a surprising one, considering the terrible shock sustained by so affectionate and so impressionable a nature.

On Monday, 6 January, and not on 7 January (one has only to reread the document to see that the confusing date of 7 January on the bottom is an error), on 6 January he had a new testament drawn up. It is claimed that the first testament (1865) was made under the influence of Mme Debacker. This time Antonio was under the influence of the family, perhaps already convinced by them to break with his companion, but did he then forget her? Granted that he left the bulk of his fortune to his natural heirs, he still reserved 150,000 francs for Mme Debacker.

He had expected that none of these cousins would console him in his grief, that they were not really close to him emotionally. He soon found this to be true. Mme Debacker, receiving the second message at Tailleville and anticipating how overwhelmed Antonio would be, left for Paris. But Antonio was surrounded by his family. He sent friends to her to negotiate a financial settlement. "I want nothing," responded Mme Debacker, "but Antonio's happiness. Let whatever he wishes be done." Strongly affected by this resignation, he yearned to blot out his memories, he lost his head, and we know the terrible scene at the fireplace to which Morel was witness.

His mind recovered quickly from this feverish attack. Every day Morel and Dr. Pasquier sent word on his progress to Mme Debacker. While Antonio's wounds healed, Morel also wrote frequently to M. Hébert. The phrasing of these letters was not discreetly softened, as is claimed; the process of recuperation may be followed there step by step. One sees the family wearying the invalid with business matters and being silenced by the doctors, the question of incompetence being debated and being similarly rejected by the doctors, and then, without an invocation of the law of 1838 even being considered, one sees Antonio entirely in charge of the administration of his affairs and giving orders to Maître Prevost to prepare for the sale of the jewelry business. [I have been unable to trace the exact identity of this "law of 1838"; its mention here presumably refers to the possibility of having Antonio comitted to an asylum.]

His mother had reserved for any child of Antonio's the ownership of the disposable portion of her estate, leaving the life estate thereof to Antonio. If the family had really thought they were dealing with a man who was in the condition they now describe, they would have kept the estate in this joint-ownership. But instead they decided to sell it by auction. [This is a complex matter, not entirely clear from what can be pieced together from the various allusions in these texts. The joint-ownership (between Antonio and any legitimate children he might eventually have) would have prevented him from disposing of that portion of his estate during his lifetime, such as by giving any part of it away to the church or to Mme Debacker. If Antonio were to die without legitimate offspring, as would be the case if he remained with Mme Debacker, he would then presumably be free to leave it to whomever he saw fit. However, in order to get their hands on the jewelry business immediately, the family agreed to permit him to liquidate it (by selling it to them). Thus, by buying the jewelry business from Antonio, the heirs did become liable to be sued by any future legitimate offspring of Antonio's, but the risk was certainly small.]

In these circumstances, Antonio encountered kinship but not sympathy. We are, they told him, your family, your cousins—but they did not speak of affection. Dr. Pasquier, whose death is certainly highly regrettable, was aware of what Antonio lacked. Antonio finally roused himself, sketched some cupids, and sent Morel with the sheet to Mme Debacker. "You will see him soon," the messenger told her. [The plaintiffs insisted that this whole episode of the cupids was a fabrication—see p. 89.] Mme Debacker, who is represented by the plaintiffs as Venus clutching her prey [*Vénus à sa proie attachée*—from Racine's *Phaedre* (1. 3. 306)], did not throw herself at Antonio; she waited. Antonio came himself to the rue Miromesnil. They then met several times at a manufacturer of artificial limbs, they took a carriage ride, they went for a stroll. That, in all its simplicity, is what falsehood has transformed into the alleged kidnapping of Antonio as he was leaving the home of a cousin.

The business was sold; Antonio's personal property was transferred to the rue Miromesnil; later, the couple left for Tailleville.

Desiring that the business should stay in the family, Antonio had publicly stipulated a minimum price of at least 200,000 francs, in order to keep other bidders away. No other buyers came forward. Furthermore, at the moment of sale, he agreed that payment might be postponed for ten years, and one of his cousins [Joseph Mellerio—pp. 94, 120] became the purchaser. The family congratulated him on this excellent arrangement, as they had congratulated Mme Debacker on her excellent nursing care. It is despicable of them to maintain now that Antonio did not return to Tailleville capable of disposing of his property, in full possession of his mental faculties, accompanied by a devoted woman.

We have seen with what clearness of mind, with what full and entire liberty, with what a persistent intention Antonio made his bequests of 1865 and January 1868. Now, with regard to the subsequent periods of the later testaments, the defense will establish, through authentic documents obtained from the heirs themselves and from close friends and family, that after Antonio's return to Tailleville his sanity and his freedom of will were never questioned, but were, on the contrary, widely recognized. The family seeks a commission of inquiry; they themselves will be the witnesses.

The relatives figuring in the case most prominently are Mme Agnel, M. Joseph Mellerio, and two others. [Mme Agnel, the only Mellerio cousin actually to visit Tailleville, was the only plaintiff who was actually an eyewitness of the ménage. Joseph Mellerio was the cousin who actually bought the jewelry business. The "two others" are presumably Jean-Antoine, who assessed the business for Joseph to buy, and Julien Forcade, who was named with Antoine (so that both sides of Antonio's family—his mother's and his father's—would thus be represented) coexecutor of Antonio's testament of 6 January 1868—p. 65. For the exact relation of these four to Antonio, see the family tree.] As for the rest of the plaintiffs, their appearance in the brief as members of the family is their first appearance in the entire affair. Thus, it is the evidence of the four principals that is most important.

With great skill Maître Pilet des Jardins divides his demonstration into a certain number of periods, according to various testaments or other acts of generosity toward Mme Debacker performed by Antonio after his recovery and his return to Tailleville, at the time when he is alleged to have been so little in control of his mental faculties, and under the sway of an irresistible tyranny. Around each of these acts the attorney groups letters and documents meant to establish the perfect independence and soundness of mind of the *de cuius*.

First period: In a testament of 4 June 1868, Antonio left half his estate to Mme Debacker. [This is not the first testament—merely the first in what Mme Debacker's attorney calls the disputed period.] Maître Pilet des Jardins reads various letters concerning family, friends, and business matters addressed at that time to Antonio from such correspondents as Mme Agnel, Dr. Pasquier, M. Morel, Maître Prevost the lawyer, which demonstrate that they knew themselves to be dealing with a man of sound mind. The testament was filed with M. Hébert, the notary. In Paris, on 27 June, Maître Prevost bid successfully, on Antonio's behalf, for several properties up for sale at auction.

Documents of this kind are equally plentiful in July.

Second period: Establishment of an annuity of 12,000 francs for Mme Debacker, through the honorable notary, Maître Hébert, on 17 September 1868. Realizing how completely a legacy is a thing of the future, Antonio wished to reassure himself of the motives for Mme Debacker's attachment to him; a legacy would bind her to him right to the end, but an annuity, whose term would begin immediately, would free her to leave him, if financial interest were in fact her only motive. The experiment satisfied Antonio: Mme Debacker remained with him. [The heirs would claim in rebuttal that successfully collecting one gift need not have prevented Mme Debacker from waiting for another—p. 90. But in the public prosecutor's summary of the case, he remarks that the annuity was given "in lieu of [Mellerio's] earlier legacies" (p. 98).]

All during the months of August, September, and October—that is to say, both before and after this establishment of an annuity—correspondence with friends and business associates continues to accumulate. These letters consist entirely of praises for Mme Debacker's care, dealings with a man of sensitive intelligence, and correspondence concerned with many and varied interests. The "religious mania" is so little in evidence that Antonio bargains about the sale of a garden with the priest of Garges, as he might with anyone. He has business dealings with M. Roger of Lisieux, who buys a property for him in Langrune. He sends receipts to Jean Mellerio, to Morel, and so on.

In December, he corresponds with the priest of Garges about masses for the repose of the soul of Mme Mellerio.

Third period: The testament of 18 June 1869. He names Mme Debacker his residuary legatee [the person inheriting everything other than certain specified exceptions], excepting only Tailleville, in which she has only the life estate; the property without life estate is bequeathed to the Convent of the Charité des Orphelines, to found an asylum for crippled paupers, to be called Saint Joseph's.

The wording of this religious legacy has been criticized. But Antonio was not a professional man of law, and this wording demonstrates, moreover, that he was not interfered with in his inspirations. We must look to his intentions, which were clearly to acknowledge the devoted attentions of Mme Debacker in proportion as they increased, and to associate this gratitude with charity to the poor.

This testament was filed, in proper fashion, with M. Hébert.

Concerning the period of this testament of 27 June—that is to say, from 2 January up to the end of June—Maître Pilet des Jardins reads an enormous number of letters, and cites numerous acts by third parties, particularly by the doctor, friends, relatives, and advisers, all of which confirm that they are dealing with a man of free will and sound mind and with a woman who is devoted to him. Antonio gaily invites his friends and relatives to come visit him at Tailleville.

Fourth period: The testament of 21 October 1869, the last. Antonio continues to name Mme Debacker his residuary legatee, but he now leaves 200,000 francs and the property of Tailleville without usufruct to the Convent of la Charité des Orphelines de la Délivrande.

The defense attorney accumulates the same kind of evidence for July, August, September, all through the rest of the year, and up to the death of Antonio in April 1870.

These documents also testify to various delicate acts of charity by Antonio on behalf of his family and friends.

He gave no sign of religious ecstasy. Nor was it only to religious establishments that he applied for servants; he made inquiries at the same time to Mme Agnel, his relative. Alone of all the relatives, she and her son Paul accepted the importunate invitations. M. Morel also visited, M. Prevost declined, Dr. Pasquier married and asked to introduce his wife. The flow of compliments to Mme Debacker never ceased.

Maître Pilet des Jardins asks if the careful examination of all these documents does not itself constitute a real commission of inquiry.

(To be continued.)

[*L'Ordre et la Liberté*, Friday, 21 June 1872]

Session of 18 June 1872 (conclusion):

We continue to summarize the argument of Maître Pilet des Jardins.

At last came Antonio's death. In order to challenge the testament, it has been alleged that this unfortunate man killed himself in a sudden fit of madness. Now, we have just seen how sound his mind really was—after the return to Tailleville there is found nothing abnormal, not even the slightest derangement. There was no fit, there was no suicide. And even supposing there was suicide after some sudden attack of unsoundness of mind, how could that invalidate a testament that already had been made six months earlier?

Antonio had just ordered a horse to be harnessed to the carriage. He had no anxieties, he was cheerful, he was

healthy. On his way upstairs to bid farewell to Mme Debacker, he continued as far as the belvedere, from which he
could see in the distance what weather to expect. The balustrade was 1.03 meters higher than the floor of the belvedere.
There has been testimony that on that day a lead roller, 8
centimeters in diameter, had been left on the platform, just
inside the balustrade, and on the side from which Antonio
fell. What happened there? Did Antonio wish to stand on
this roller, with nothing higher than the balustrade of 95
centimeters (103 minus 8) for support? Did he lean forward
too far, to see the carriage or some other object of his attention? And then—tall and strong, but with both hands
mutilated— did he lose his balance? This is the most plausible explanation. There were no witnesses. Richer, the gardener, saw Antonio fall, but only as he reached the ground.

In his testament made at the time of the death of Mme
Mellerio, with which the family was familiar, he had named
his cousins [Antoine Mellerio and Julien Forcade] executors.
At the news of Antonio's death, they came running, and
found Mme Debacker overwhelmed with grief; she told them
of the last testament, in her favor; they declared that they
would not accept it, they reproached her with her past, on
which they said they were relying to bring suit—they, mil-
lionaires, against her, a woman without resources and without support; they forced from her the settlement that has
been brought to the Court's attention and in which they included, in an offhand way, as if it were of no great importance, the phrase "some eccentricities," a phrase on which
they are now attempting to capitalize.

Later the settlement fell through, on account of the refusal
by M. Debacker, whose role in this affair has indeed been
peculiar, to give his legal consent. [M. Debacker, though he
did not wish to share his own fortune with his wife, apparently did not wish to see her unduly impoverished by someone else.]

Mme Debacker has been called greedy, and yet here we see
her, inheriting millions but nevertheless willing to settle for
an annuity of 12,000 francs. After Antonio's death as well as
before it, cupidity was clearly never her motive.

The plaintiffs have tried to use in their argument an account of the event that appeared in a little local newspaper [the *Bonhomme Normand*] and to infer from it some kind of public notoriety. The style of reporting employed in that story is deplorable.

Private misfortunes cannot be understood by such methods of inquiry. Interpretations of suicide and worse were immediately offered as the plain truth, without hesitation or verification. Now generally, when confronted with a corpse, people do not indulge so easily in such lurid stories and wild charges. Public gossip could hardly have furnished to the newspaper that version and that commentary, so misleading and so favorable to the cousins, concerning the terrible incineration of Antonio's hands. And not only did the newspaper account distort the situation of Mme Debacker, it went on to cast aspersions on both religion in general and the Convent of la Délivrande in particular. This abuse of the press could be nothing other than a deliberate act of the Mellerio family; it could only have been they who sent, or arranged to have sent, to the newspaper these false rumors, which could be started with such lamentable ease. Mellerio heirs, you are the source of those stories, fabricating then that same "public opinion" that you are invoking today.

Richer, the honest and devoted gardener of Tailleville, who saw how calm his master was as he climbed up to the belvedere and who would a few moments later see him crash to the earth, sent to the paper a denial that was published in the following issue. It is claimed that in so doing he was obeying the directions of Mme Debacker. But if financial interest rather than love of truth had been his motive, it would not have been with Mme Debacker that he would have thought it profitable to side.

The newspaper article and the papers obtained from the lawyer, Maître Prevost, did not satisfy the heirs. They now claim a deficit in the estate of 300,000 francs. But Mme Debacker rejects their figures and their base suspicions. A correct calculation of the estate shows a deficit of no more than 7,000 francs, which easily may have been consumed in miscellaneous details.

Another reason the Mellerios would like a commission of inquiry is no doubt to enable them to produce Morel, the family financial agent—Morel, who thanked Mme Debacker for her good care of Antonio. But it is not worth the trouble. The situation is already quite clear.

The plaintiffs have gone so far into trivial details as to invoke Mme Debacker's dismissal of an old servant woman. But two memorandums in the inventory prove that it was Antonio who personally settled her account, and that she was not dismissed in destitution.

Among the eccentricities with which Antonio's memory is being charged is that one day he buried the meat meant for dinner, under the pretext that meat should not be eaten at Tailleville that day, and that he then went off to eat meat at Courcelles. Now, this episode actually had to do with rotten meat that the servants had tried to feed to the dogs, against his orders. The Mellerio account at the butcher who supplied this meat was cut off that very day. Just see what constructions are placed on such events!

Then appears one of the lodgers at Tailleville, a M. Jousse. He was a strolling musician along the nearby beaches whom Antonio happened to encounter one day. With all the man's family hungry to the point of starvation, Antonio sent them to help themselves at the kitchen table. Jousse, who had more than one string to his bow, was then hired to restore the paintings in the château. He also has evidence to give. In fact, in a letter which Maître Allou has not hesitated to read in court, this bohemian "offers" to testify that, at Tailleville, Antonio and Mme Debacker led the life of the damned. If one has many such witnesses, it is understandable that a commission of inquiry would be desirable. One can sometimes arrange to have so many things emerge in a commission of inquiry! But since the case is sufficiently clear already, Mme Debacker refuses to step into this trap toward which the plaintiffs would lead her.

Finally, there is what has been called the affidavit of Dr. Pasquier. It is painful to see such a document come from the hand of a close friend of Antonio's, a man with such affection for Mme Debacker, a man who, fallen so bravely at Neuilly, does command a certain respect. The affidavit contradicts the doctor's own letters and conduct right up to Antonio's death. Moreover, he gives accounts of events that he did not witness, he labels Antonio's death as a suicide, and he infers therefrom a whole chain of acts of insanity. But did Antonio commit suicide?

The Court is adjourned and will reconvene tomorrow, Wednesday.

Session of June 19

Maître Pilet des Jardins concludes his remarks.

He returns to the Pasquier affidavit. He deplores the fact that the doctor should have decided to write such a document with litigation in the offing, and to have been so rashly opinionated without more complete information.

The terms employed in this document concerning Mme Debacker depart from the claims of both truth and proper medical verification, and they contradict the benevolent terms of the letters of the same Dr. Pasquier concerning the defendant.

This is not the only contradiction.

The doctor speaks of an erotic delirium after Antonio's fit of fever following the cold bath of October 1867; to cure this "eroticism," he took the singular remedy of sending the invalid to Mme Debacker at Tailleville.

The affidavit relates this attack of fever in 1867 to the alleged suicide of 1870. How? Through some series of psychological links? No, it makes no attempt at the slightest connection.

The doctor witnessed nothing. Interested parties spoke to him of suicide, and he based his conclusions on an event he was not personally familiar with—they are not admissible as evidence.

It has been claimed that Mme Debacker seized Antonio as her prey. Now, the affidavit of Dr. Pasquier, who did know about that, attests that, on the contrary, it was Antonio who returned to her. This should not be forgotten.

The affidavit does not hesitate to charge an honorable ecclesiastic and two pious nuns with having improperly urged Antonio, at his mother's bedside, to promise to change his life, and it tries to link this alleged pressure to the horrible scene of the hand-burning. Do the heirs forget that at that time Antonio was so little insane that he made the testament of 6 January, leaving nearly his entire estate to his heirs, naming his two cousins MM. A. Mellerio and Forcade executors, and only giving Mme Debacker 150,000 francs? They do not see, then, under whose influence Antonio could have been at that time, if not theirs?

Unsoundness of mind is displayed not merely by the entertainment of wild ideas but by mental alteration brought about by the shock of a crisis. There is found to be no continuity in the reasoning process, no logic. Ideas are totally changed, affections become dislikes; there is a complete mental reversal: psychologists [*les alienistes*] confirm this.

Now, with Antonio we find nothing of the kind, during the seventeen years in which he knew Mme Debacker. He never left her except at an extraordinary moment, the death of his mother; and he soon returned to her, reaffirming his feelings for her through a series of unambiguous acts.

The testament has been attacked on the grounds of unsoundness of mind: yes, he was admittedly mad during the terrible scene following the death of his mother. But then he promptly recovered, as is verified by the letters from Morel to Maître Hébert; and his correspondence, his public acts, the final settlement of 180,000 francs [the price of the jewelry business] with the cousins, all the documents submitted to the Court, particularly those belonging to the period of the last testament—all prove that he enjoyed the free exercise of his mental powers.

The testament has also been attacked on the grounds of undue influence. Now, none of the fraudulent maneuvers that constitute undue influence can be found in this case. [For a full definition of undue influence, see the summary of the public prosecutor, p. 100.] Antonio is seen to have always been entirely free, both in thought and in deed; and if friends other than Morel and relatives other than Mme Agnel and her son Paul did not come to Tailleville to see this for themselves, it was not for want of being invited and finding the door open.

The fiction has been invented that, on the occasion of Antonio's return to the rue Miromesnil, Mme Debacker exclaimed [to representatives of his family], "Where would I be with your 12,000 annuity—I would be wretchedly poor! But now I have him, and he will not escape me again!" Mme Debacker repudiates this fabrication. If Morel had heard any such thing, he would hardly have sent her his compliments in a letter to Antonio a few days later.

The plaintiffs have claimed that Mme Mellerio cursed Mme Debacker, with whom her son lived a most quiet and orderly life.

The plaintiffs have also claimed that Antonio's wardrobe was in a ruinous condition. The entries in the inventory belie this falsehood.

The plaintiffs have made the outrageous assertion that Mme Debacker was previously the mistress of M. de Mongino; this is pure slander.

The plaintiffs have claimed that she exploited religion, that she manipulated Antonio by means of a false piety; this period of rehabilitating Antonio through charity has been smeared with the name of hypocrisy. "You have introduced into the debate an Anna de Beaupré," cries the orator passionately. "I forbid you to introduce a Lady Tartuffe!" [The hero of Moliere's *Tartuffe,* or *L'Imposteur,* was a sensual religious hypocrite who insinuated himself into his victim's household, becoming wealthy at the family's expense.]

A Father Joseph has also been introduced, who is said to have influenced Antonio by threatening him with hell. But where? When? Who is this Father Joseph? There is someone by this common name to be found in many religious establishments, both in France and abroad. Where is the one of Tailleville?

The defendants are the ones who are accumulating evidence in this argument before the Court. The plaintiffs, who wish the Court to order a commission of inquiry, have up to now been able to produce only a useless list of allegations.

Counsel brings to the Court's attention a judgment of the Court of Agen, dated 7 May 1850, together with various appellate decisions, all denying a commission of inquiry in similar cases.

He persists in maintaining that Antonio, "who was all heart" ["*qui n'était qu'un coeur*"], had shown by successive acts with regard to Mme Debacker that his intentions were generous, fixed, and independent. Even in the testament made under the stress of his mother's death, and surrounded by his family, he did not forget her.

During seventeen years, by whom was he loved? By Mme

Debacker. During seventeen years, whom did he love? Mme Debacker—first for her beauty, and then for her devoted affection when his cousins abandoned him.

His concern for the poor is virtuous and laudable religion, not excessive religiosity. The poor are already found in his testament of June 1869, where Tailleville, "his dear child," is destined for them. First Mme Debacker is to continue there her works of charity, and after her death it will belong completely to the poor.

Their share increases yet again in the testament of the following October.

Mme Debacker and the poor: these are his legatees.

The Court will uphold his final testament, the testament of 21 October 1869; it will uphold it without a commission of inquiry because the liberty and soundness of mind of the testator are verified more than amply by the facts of the case.

The Court will recall the letter concerning this testament written by Antonio to Maître Prevost, who was then trying to dissuade him from making these legacies:

"I am only doing my duty as an honorable man by naming Anna to be my legatee and to continue my work—Anna, who is with me, who cares for me, who gives me her life. . . . If I were married and had children, would my cousins be my legatees? No, of course not. And so, since I will not marry, I adopt the poor as my children." [This letter, of 10 August 1869, was held by the court to be crucial in establishing the rationality of Mellerio's testament of 21 October 1869. For the full quotation of the relevant passage, cited in the text of the court's judgment, see p. 121.]

And the Court will respect these last wishes, this fixed resolve, so clearly expressed.

The floor is given to Maître Carel, counsel for the Convent.

(To be continued.)

[*L'Ordre et la Liberté*, Saturday, 22 June 1872]

Session of 19 June 1872

The attempt we have been making to summarize these legal arguments, as faithfully as our inadequacy will permit, becomes at this point even more difficult. It is not that the rhetoric of Maître Carel is unattractive—on the contrary—but this sort of argument is not of the kind that can be easily reproduced from mere notes, more or less abridged, taken rapidly and then quickly copied. Choice expressions, lofty thoughts, eloquent periods, charming style—in a word, all the great rhetorical qualities, disappear, alas! in a summary *résumé* that often retains—and then only in an incomplete fashion—merely the dry points of an arid argument, and in place of oratory offers nothing but explication.

Maître Carel really must pardon us for this mutilation, which we do not perform without sincere regret. But as would be expected, considering both his talent and the client he was defending, his eloquence was so impressive that, no matter how inadequately it may be reproduced, it is bound to have its effect.

Thus, our readers will understand why, even beyond the exceptionally large fortune at stake and the fame of the lawyers, and without prejudging in any way the outcome of the case, we had decided from the very first, without doubt or hesitation, in the midst of all the gossip that has been swirling about this case, to impose on ourselves the heavy task—but also the duty—of recording at length such complex arguments.

Here, then, in brief, are Maître Carel's remarks:

The establishment which he represents is named "the Convent of Notre Dame de la Charité des Orphelines de Marie de la Délivrande." It dates from 1825. Its original charter charges the Convent with providing for indigent girls, and also with maintaining a boardinghouse for girls and an asylum for the sick. These sisters lead not the mystical life of a contemplative order but the active life of good works. Here orphans, little girls "who have no longer any mother," find devoted substitutes. The foundation was originally located in Bayeux.

In 1833 the then Mother Superior, Mlle Henriette d'Osseville, established [at Douvres] the Convent of la Délivrande, whose separate and independent existence was ratified by a decree of 1853.

Mlle d'Osseville and her family devoted several hundred thousand francs to this work of charity. Nature had not favored physically this pious and benevolent woman; the wonderful tendency of the human heart that disposes us to take special pity on those whose sufferings we ourselves have experienced led her to add to her hospital an orthopedic center, where good care could provide deformed children with the physical advantages nature had denied them.

A small establishment by the sea completed the hygienic and curative facilities of the Convent.

These details are relevant; perhaps they determined the direction of Antonio Mellerio's generosity, since he was himself mutilated. In any case, it is in regard to this generosity that we must determine whether there has been, as Maître Allou has put it with a heavily emphasized moderation [p. 38], a moderate modernation to which the speaker pays moderate respects, a "less than shameless use of undue influence."

To Mlle d'Osseville succeeded Mme Dauger, an equally noble woman. This current Mother Superior has also given generously . . . but the speaker will not divulge the exact amount, since the donor is still alive.

The Convent has had several branches founded. Together with the head office, they provide maintenance and education for 500 orphan girls.

The Convent of la Délivrande has as its religious director the honorable Abbé Leconte, the parish priest of Sainte-Trinité at Falaise.

The Convent is cloistered—that is to say, cut off from ordinary relations with the world.

With M. Mellerio their relations were as infrequent as they were insignificant; with Mme Debacker they had none.

Before the testament of October 1869, the Convent sent to M. Mellerio, as they did to all prosperous landowners of the region, a request to buy some tickets in a charitable lottery. After the testament there were just two letters, in February 1870. M. Mellerio had dismissed Amélie, one of his servants, and, as has already been remarked, he made several inquiries to find a replacement for her. In the Convent's parlor he said a few words on the subject to the housekeeper. He later wrote to her, seeking a cook. On 23 February the housekeeper sent him a note asking for details about the position. Antonio answered, giving the age desired and the salary offered. On the following Sunday he came by to say in person that he had already settled the affair.

There we have all the facts of the case—nothing more, nothing less. One request to buy lottery tickets, and an exchange of two letters for a service never rendered.

In April 1870 the Mother Superior first heard about a legacy involving the beautiful estate of Tailleville and a sum of 200,000 francs. The legatees were the orphans; the Convent understood that it was chosen solely as a medium for charity. Only in the testament of October 1869 was the Convent actually named, but in that of June of the same year, with the same intention though with less felicity in legal terminology, M. Mellerio had made his charitable views manifest.

The first measures the nuns took were very conservative. Their attorney made careful arrangements to be present at the drawing up of the inventory. There had been so little intrigue, and this legacy was so little expected, that they were unfamiliar with the situation and hesitant to take risks. This circumspection should be emphasized, not for blame but for praise. What little they knew of Mellerio was entirely superficial. Under what circumstances had he acted, was he sick or healthy, was he independent or under some unknown influence? They had to be cautious; it was their duty, especially in the case of a man whose life had been ended by an accident so variously interpreted. But if the testator did prove to be mentally independent, if they in fact were the object of a pious and legal generosity, it was their duty to defend the gift, regardless of whatever easy suspicions and recriminations—of the sort that so often accompany charitable legacies—there might be.

Thus, caution was necessary; and if it was necessary for a long time, the fault is not the Convent's but in fact the plaintiffs', who did not deliver their list of allegations to the secondary party [the convent] until three days before the hearing, and to the principal party [Mme Debacker] only after their opening speech.

So, the Convent asks flatly that the arrogant demand of the Mellerio heirs for nullification be dismissed, together with all the allegations that they bring forward.

70

The plaintiffs have tried to imply some peculiar relationship between the Convent and the château of Tailleville. But in vain.

They have also spoken of the testator's unsoundness of mind, that is to say, of a mental condition that did not permit Antonio Mellerio to be fully conscious of the testamentary acts he performed. They have leaned heavily, though moderately [another sneer at Maître Allou], on the question of unsoundness of mind, or, more to the legal point, on the question of fraudulent maneuvers (*des manoeuvres dolosives*) that would have led the testator to make bequests other than those he would have made had he not been under the influence of criminal suggestion.

The illustrious counsel for the Mellerio heirs claims to have chosen to take a position of relative moderation, but, indeed, the case requires him to.

The plaintiffs have not dared to ask for an absolute annulment of the testament. Can it be that in all their piles of evidence there is not one piece that permits them to attain their goal directly? They are obliged to admit that all those documents together do not amount to the evidence that they seek. And thus they wish to search for it in the extreme expedient of an commission of inquiry.

For all their emphasis on unsoundness of mind, the plaintiffs have not taken that as their principal charge; they have conceded that without undue influence, which is to say, without fraudulent maneuvers, if Antonio had been alone or at least free of the influences that are supposed to have been brought to bear on him, he would have been, as in the case of his business affairs with his relatives, sufficiently competent to have made a testament. They have settled for claiming that, weakened by emotional shocks, he fell prey to intrigue. The plea of unsoundness of mind disappears into innuendo (*la nuance*), and turns into a plea of undue influence. Such a strategy is called abandoning a forward position to take up one in the rear, and to be fighting a battle while already in retreat. And in this way, we eventually reach a charge of mere suggestion.

A third concession has been made. Antonio was originally described as having been an erotic maniac for twenty-five years, after which an emotional shock then turned him into a religious maniac. It is apparently true that it is possible for such a thing to happen. But now when his youth is discussed he is only said to have indulged in "follies," and even of such "follies" only one can be displayed from his last or even his two last years.

Fourth concession: it has been admitted that this mania that has been so grotesquely exaggerated did not grip him in his ordinary affairs of family and business. No, he is said to have fallen prey to an over-excitement of the most beautiful of all sentiments, the religious sentiment. This finally is the only position left to the plaintiffs. And does even this occur every day of his life, every hour? One has only to read Antonio's correspondence to be convinced of the contrary. Even this is nothing more than intermittent. What a point to be reduced to!

The plaintiffs turn to invoke previous disorders. But if those had enfeebled his spirit, they ought also to have weakened his body, if there really is a relation between the physical and mental faculties. But, on the contrry, he enjoyed vigorous health. *Mens sana in corpore sano.*

The life at Tailleville did not depress him. He seemed to be determined to repair what he had destroyed in mutilating himself. This man had no hands, he had only stumps; and with them and his mouth, through great perseverance, he wrote, and even drew. In his drawings the idea of the beautiful may be discerned—nothing gross, nothing animal. There may not always be found in them purity of line, but always pure are the conceptions and compositions that come—how else can it be put—from his lips!

It is truly a resurrection!

Here is this weakened man, displaying such great energy; here is an aesthetic blossom, often perhaps without fruit, but demonstrating to every eye the vigor and vitality of its sap.

If this portrait be just, there is no unsoundness of mind to be found in it, and the testament is valid. Nor can it be claimed that the portrait displays the trait of religious frenzy—the testament is purely and simply a reasonable act of charity, of which both the birth and growth may be traced.

"The first of my colleagues," adds Maître Carel, "has said, 'I will be a witness.' The second has responded, 'The facts themselves will bear witness,' and contented himself with the role of advocate. Permit me, Sirs, to usurp your function for one moment, and to judge."

The *de cuius* died *integri status*—that is, in full possession of his legal capacities. When a person's mental faculties are discovered to be deranged, most families are concerned to hide it. As long as the possibility remains, the spouse or parent or son or nearest relation has himself given power of attorney by the person whose reason is abandoning him. The situation is thus kept veiled from the public as long as possible.

The Mellerios were not so delicate. After the death of Antonio's mother, and the fit that followed it, the family was apparently of one mind concerning his mental condition. They even entertained the notion of having him declared incompetent. But we have seen while considering the invalid's recovery, a quite prompt recovery whose progress may be traced in Morel's letters, that the doctors rejected this plan.

If at that time or later Antonio did not enjoy the full exercise of his mental powers, it was the family's duty, especially considering his new financial situation, to take every possible legal and humane step to protect him, either by having him committed to an institution or by taking the less radical measure, when his mind was not completely clouded, of appointing a guardian for him.

Now, we have seen that the Mellerios are not given to hanging back (*reculer*). If they did nothing, it was only because they could do nothing.

They prove by their own acts that they considered their relative completely capable of handling financial affairs.

For instance, as will be remembered through numerous repetitions in these pleadings, in her testament Mme Mellerio had entailed her real and personal property; fully half that estate was vested in the present or future children of Antonio, who himself had only a life interest in that portion. Now, keep in mind that the family did not take a single one of the aforementioned precautions concerning this situation, and also that the joint heirship prevented any of the property from being conveyed to others. But nevertheless, the family appointed a trustee for the entailed portion of the estate—not for Antonio—in order to hold an auction, and to that end the family themselves, in contradiction of the very grounds on which they now dare to bring the present suit, the family themselves gave that entailed portion of the estate to the man on whose soundness of mind they now cast doubt.

This event is not trivial; its prominence in the case is extremely significant.

Thus we see that Antonio did have the capacity for business dealings, and that the family realized it; they acted fairly, they acted well. And if they were to assert the contrary today, they would be slandering themselves for the sake of winning their suit.

What acts during these years is the *de cuius* not seen accomplishing? He receives his rents and interest and revenue, he orders goods, he pays out money, he keeps precise accounts. He settles major business affairs with Morel and three members of the Mellerio family (May and December 1869). [The first date is presumably that of the sale of the jewelry business (although a year later, in its brief summary of the appeal, *L'Ordre et la Liberté* gives the date of the business sale as 24 April 1868), and the second is the granting of a ten-year delay of payment.] He disposes of property, not only in the important sale of the business to his family, but also in the sale of a garden to the priest of Garges, and property in Langrune to M. Roger (from Lisieux); he borrows money from M. Bourdon; he deals with M. Mauger—and all these dealings are negotiated over considerable distance and with men of irreproachable integrity.

If we inquire into his personal relationships, they withstand examination equally well. An insane person characteristically forgets his personal ties, or at least neglects the proprieties. But Antonio's behavior and his correspondence both display a perfect tact, and the amenities are never overlooked. One letter, sent to the operatic singer Roger (mutilated, like himself) concerning the shipment of a portrait Antonio had done of him, contains a delicate allusion. His correspondence with a music editor is charming. He writes to M. Pilet des Jardins, who was his friend, though never a companion in his revels, and he consults him in his capacity as an attorney. When he writes to Morel, the tone changes; it is now one appropriate for use with an old friend of the family. If Antonio is corresponding with the priest at Garges, the style is in accordance with the subject, whether it concerns masses for the repose of Mme Mellerio's soul or the sale of a garden. On every occasion the style is appropriate for the correspondent and the circumstances. The most perfect decorum is always preserved.

The same sensitivity is apparent in his gifts, in his generosity toward his family, his friends, his servants.

His relations with his family are irreproachable. He agrees to sell them the business. He stipulates that they may take ten years to pay, not only for the goodwill but also for the considerable value of the jewels themselves. There is a letter from one of his relations praising him for this action. They were eager [*ils s'empressèrent*] to accept this favor, from which they continue to profit at this very moment, and yet they now dare to declare him unfit to conduct business, and to attack him on those very grounds!

If he writes to Joseph Mellerio, he speaks of business matters where appropriate and of family matters where appropriate. If he writes to Mme Agnel, he talks of such matters as music, painting, and travel. He invites her to visit Tailleville. We know that he even discussed his charitable projects with her, because—and the Court is begged to take note of this detail—in one of her last letters Mme Agnel asks him, "And what about the poor?" He is generous to Louis Mellerio; he is a benefactor of Jacques's widow [see the family tree in the Appendix].

And does the family seek further evidence? There is much more available. They themselves have more letters and personal documents that only they know the contents of, and yet they do not bring forward a single one—and the reason is that in this material there is not one word of insanity, not one word from which it could possibly be inferred that the *de cuius* had been under any influence of any kind.

Schemers typically swarm around rich men known to be easy prey. But nothing of the sort has been shown to have happened with Antonio, although he was not kept in seclusion but rather received friends and circulated with complete freedom of movement. So no one considered this man of opulent wealth as prey. This is an important piece of common knowledge.

He had advisors, attorneys, and agents, all men of well-deserved high repute, competence, and complete integrity—in Douvres, Maître Hébert, and in Paris, Morel, Marichal, and Maître Prevost.

Antonio wrote first drafts of more than one hundred highly personal letters in his brother Victor's notebook. [This notebook of first drafts covered the last several months of Mellerio's life. There is some question of its exact span of coverage: the public prosecutor mentions "ten months" (June 1869 to April 1870) and "200 letters" (p. 112); but in a portion of the appeal arguments not included in this collection, Maître Carel (again the convent's attorney) more specifically refers to 154 letters dating from June through December 1869 (*Journal de Caen*, 20 July 1873). This notebook was vital to the defendants' success, not only in the trial, for establishing Mellerio's capacity to do business, but also in the appeal, for reducing the charges of forgery to absurdity: since the handwriting of the notebook was the same as that of the testament, the heirs were compelled to insist that even the first drafts had been forged (pp. 161–62.)] Whether those letters concern business affairs, family, friends, or whatever, there is nothing to be found in them but good sense. "Read them, Messieurs," says Maître Carel to the Court, "read them, I beg you. That will be an interrogation of this man whose memory is being slandered. And the examination will enable you to dispense with the motion for an commission of inquiry that is being made against him."

Proceeding to Antonio's testaments, we find his acts performed in the most personal possible way, which is to say, the way which most inspires confidence that they were the work of the testator himself. He wrote them personally, with his mouth.

Concerning the testament of 4 June 1868, the notary at Douvres certified having witnessed it, and this public official, whose duty it is to ensure that the testaments filed with him are authentic, found this one to have been filed under conditions so sensible and irreproachable that he contented himself simply with certifying that he had witnessed it, and placing it on file.

This testament of June 1869 was merely filed, not drawn up formally. Antonio was no legal expert [*jurisconsulte*], and it is possible that he inadequately expressed his charitable intentions. But those intentions are obviously there, and no amount of quasi-legal libel can make them disappear.

When opinion of counsel was sought concerning the validity of this version, a new draft was suggested. Possibly, indeed probably, a model was requested from Maître Hébert, the notary, who had Antonio's confidence; and Maître Hébert had no reason to refuse, since he had a very clear grasp of the situation. He drew up a legal draft for a man whose resolve was fixed.

Was Antonio's generosity exaggerated? That is not the question at issue here. Besides its judicial power, there are such matters as equity, proper limits, proportion; the State does have the power to make reasonable adjustments in excessively generous gifts. But exaggeration does not require nullification. The Orphanage of la Délivrande will know what course to take should this issue be brought up before the competent authorities.

What we have here is an act on which the testator has reflected for months, an act whose legal phraseology was obtained from an honest and disinterested friend, an act whose proposal was submitted to Maître Prevost, attacked by him and then defended by Antonio. During that period Mme Agnel was at Tailleville and Maître Prevost was invited to visit. Antonio acted freely and of his own accord, with a perfect understanding of what he was doing; he has left on record his motives. It was not the Convent that he had in mind, but the poor, his children. He clearly intended his act, he was a free agent, he acted legally, and justice will uphold that act.

Most of the plaintiffs know personally that he was in fact competent. Many had very important dealings with him. Perhaps Maître Prevost happened to mention to them a few words about this proposed testament, concerning which he was not, after all, sworn to secrecy. Mme Agnel must have known something: "And what about the poor?" she asked. And not one of these presumably watchful heirs found the slightest opportunity to say of Antonio while he was alive, "This man is mad," and to take steps to prevent his making a testament.

Antonio died in April 1870, falling from his belvedere. He had had an attack of fever in 1867, and the death of his mother threw him into a terrible fit of delirium in 1868. After that—nothing. Efforts have been made, without a shred of proof, to relate the event on the belvedere to these two crises and to derive thereby not an accident but a suicide. The question of suicide is completely irrelevant to the case; it would not invalidate the charitable legacy made freely and with full competency in October 1869. It would have been better for the family to throw a veil over such an unhappy ending of a Mellerio.

They have succeeded no better with the eccentricities that they seek to lay at Antonio's door. In the testament there is not a single trace of religious mania, nothing that displays the slightest influence on the smallest bequest. The testament is free [*vierge*] of any kind of religious mania; it is purely and simply a work of charity.

After his prompt recovery following the death of his mother, Antonio Mellerio regained full possession of himself, with all his characteristics and faults. Although his nature was impulsive and demonstrative, he was none the less entirely in possession of his mental faculties and completely master of his will. He bequeathed his estate, voluntarily and after a hostile inquiry into his act, to the orphanage. The Convent does not hesitate to ask that his testament be executed.

There has been a charge of undue influence. And thus the Convent, not even aware it was a legatee until the testament was read, finds itself obliged to defend itself against such a charge.

Was it alone or in complicity that the Convent is supposed to have become guilty of undue influence—shameless or not, yet always shameful? [*Ehontée ou non, mais toujours honteuse*—the allusion to shamelessness refers to Maître Allou's closing comment that "there was no shameless undue influence on the part of the Convent" (p. 50).]

A small amount of insignificant correspondence from some foreign persons or religious orders to the Convent has been cited. From the Convent itself only three letters have been brought forward.

The plaintiffs submit neither facts nor documents. They are satisfied with allegations, with accusing a religious order of undue influence; in other words, they are making a deplorable appeal to prejudice. There is correspondence between Antonio and tradesmen, friends, and family; but between Tailleville and the Convent there is nothing but one circular for lottery tickets and, five months after the testament, two banal letters concerning a service that M. Mellerio also requested from his cousin Mme Agnel and that events did not permit to be rendered. No, no! Undue influence, fraudulent maneuvers—these are nowhere to be found.

A Father Joseph who has been mentioned has still to be identified. And even if he were identified, there would be no connection between him and the Convent, or between his doings and the charitable legacy [because, whoever he may have been, as a priest he must have been connected with the Missionary Fathers of la Délivrande, not with the Convent].

In any event, the inhabitants of the Convent cannot have worked at influencing Antonio; they are cloistered—no one could have gone to Tailleville. And Mellerio did not come to the Convent except on one or two occasions several months after the testament was filed. And then his letters and visits were hardly those of a man posing as a benefactor. The Convent dealt with him casually, as a person with an ordinary problem of domestic service.

So much for direct undue influence.

A charge of indirect undue influence holds up under examination no better. The Convent did not sway him by obtaining him servants, either before or after the testament. The head of the Order lives in Falaise. No contact at all can be found through the Missionary Fathers of la Délivrande. Through Mme Debacker—the plaintiffs have dared to insinuate that through her there was contact. Yet not a fact, not a single word, to support such insolence!

And surely an obstacle to such an association, from the Convent's point of view, would have been the fact that Mme Debacker was, of all persons, the least interested in lending herself to such a project. An earlier testament had left her the entire estate. This one would take from her 600,000 francs, which was at least half of that estate. This fact alone is sufficient to demonstrate that from her side the allegation is inadmissible.

"As for the Convent," adds Maître Carel (as nearly as we could manage to record his words *verbatim*), "I plead for an honorable religious establishment, whose director is equally honorable. I plead in the name of women grown old in the service of God and the poor—against the accusation that for money Mme Dauger put her hand into that of Mme Debacker. I need not defend my client against such an allegation.

"And meanwhile you, my honorable opponent, you, with the clear conscience, you, the master of oratory—your clients have whispered to you that such connivance might have existed, you have charged the Convent with undue influence, and you have said that it would not have been shameless!

"So, our sisters and daughters, in exchange for their renunciation of the joys of this world, in exchange for the sacrifice of their freedom, in exchange for the aversions inherent in their ministry of healing—our daughters, our sisters, who, at the call of religion, have abandoned our hearths to dedicate themselves to the great family of the poor, to raise, succor, and instruct young orphan girls, to serve as sisters and mothers to the little children of a people who often, deplorably incited against religious orders, insult them, alas! and often even murder them—these noble women are made targets of public suspicion, and any millionaire who cares to can drag them through the public courts and force them to defend themselves against incredible accusations, and it is accepted as entirely natural!

"Sirs, you shall be satisfied—the Mother Superior of the Convent des Orphelines de la Charité de Notre Dame de la Délivrande, laying aside for the moment the humility and calm of her cloister, presents herself before you, sustained by the respect of the entire region; strong in her indisputable honor and her impeccable life, she rises before you in this 'immaculate robe' at which you have jeered—and for her entire defense she answers you, 'I am Mme Dauger.' " ["*Je suis Dauger.*"]

Then, addressing the judges, the speaker concludes:

"You can see, your honors, we are in the right, We have the

80

truth on our side. You represent justice, integrity, and the support of our most sacred rights. We await your judgment with confidence."

In spite of the solemnity of the place, scattered applause greeted the splendid peroration of this splendid orator.

The Court was adjourned, with the rebuttals deferred until the continuation of the session. We will publish an equally full account of them, for they too are worthy of close study.

[*L'Ordre et la Liberté*, Sunday, 23 June]

Session of 19 June 1872

(Continued)

At the reopening of the session, Maître Allou begins his rebuttal. We continue to summarize:

In every lawsuit the moment arrives when secondary considerations must give way to primary ones. This case has reached that point.

The speaker considers that he was extremely moderate, in his appraisal of the facts and their significance, in his consideration of the questions of undue influence and unsoundness of mind, and in his request for a commission of inquiry in order to clarify the issues of the case. This moderation has been praised, but it has also been abused. It has been construed as an admission that the undue influence and unsoundness of mind were merely slight, and by seizing on these two alleged concessions, the conclusion has been drawn, with Strafford, that:

"From two white horses you cannot make a black one."

For his only response to the intemperate and highly colored rhetoric that has so recently been admired, Maître Allou wishes to return the argument to the plain facts of the case and to the real meaning of the proposed commission of inquiry. He never meant to imply that Antonio was mad enough to require a straitjacket [*fou à lier*], but he does maintain that a demonstrable unsoundness of mind, though not actually lunacy, kept Antonio from that full independence of mind that is required for a legitimate testator. Likewise for undue influence: although there is no one single conclusive

81

proof, Antonio was nevertheless constrained in such a way that his expression of will could not be what it would have been had such constraint not been applied.

There is no need to cite decisions of the Court of Agen or the *Cour de Cassation* [the highest court of appeal in France]. There are no real precedents for a case of this sort— it is for the judges alone to decide. [There is some truth in this argument that precedents were lacking. In fact, the only reason that the full text of the court's judgment in this case is still available is that the annual collection of the decisions of the Courts of Appeal of Caen and Rouen considered this case to be so important that they went to the extraordinary length of including the full text of the original judgment in their record of the 1873 appeal—see the headnote to chapter 4.] Theirs is the power. It is up to them to decide if the state of mind of the *de cuius* and the situation in which he lived permit the assumption that he acted in full possession of his faculties and that there is no need for a commission of inquiry.

If the concessions the speaker has made on these subjects have been abused, he hereby retracts them. He will now take a position more intransigent, though still by no means unreasonable.

When he made his testaments, was Antonio free and sound of mind? The speaker does not wish to deny it absolutely, nor would he ever be led to such exaggeration by the interests confided to him. But the extravagances with which the *de cuius* is reproached give rise to considerable doubt on the question, and constitute sufficiently serious grounds for presumption of unsoundness of mind to justify a request for a commission of inquiry in order to satisfy everyone concerned.

Certainly, the Court should exercise great care in granting petitions for a commission of inquiry; and in a case where the truth shone forth clearly, it would be pointless to search for further evidence. But in the type of case under consideration here, the heirs have made the concession of not positively affirming Antonio's insanity, but they nevertheless insist that there do exist serious, specific and interrelated grounds for ordering a commission of inquiry. This is not a strategy dictated by weakness, it is the occupation of a truly impregnable position.

Was Antonio free and sound of mind? That is the question to be decided.

Neither of the defendants has even touched on the issue of Antonio's hallucinations, nor on any of those aspects that, in the hands of a speaker less moderate than the present one, would be grounds for a suit for *de plano* nullification of the testament.

The master of Tailleville was a colossus, indeed, but a colossus shaken by the storm; an athlete, if you will, but an athlete in weakened condition, both physically and mentally.

Maître Allou does not accuse him of inebriation in the vulgar sense of the word. But unhappily Antonio had discovered an elegant inebriation, often no less dangerous than the other kind, in the world of the young bloods of Paris. He yielded himself up to it, as he no doubt also yielded himself up to gambling, and as he yielded himself up to the worst inebriation of all-that of the voluptuary.

It has been claimed that in writing to Victor he accused himself of his brother's faults in order to teach him a lesson, no doubt as in Sparta drunken slaves were displayed in the street in order to disgust the children with this degrading vice; and the conclusion has been drawn, on behalf of Mme Debacker, that those lascivious details are present in the letters only in order to preach morality. This is surely an excessively broad interpretation.

By nature energetic, Antonio drifted toward violence; his mind was not prepared for a shock, but a shock came in October 1867 [the fever after the cold bath]. Dr. Pasquier eventually managed to calm his delirium, but we now hear cries of: why did he then send Antonio to Tailleville, where Mme Debacker was residing? The facts of the matter are that the doctor certainly recommended sending Antonio to breathe the pure country air at Tailleville, but he never meant for Mme Debacker to be there too. Indeed, he ordered the contrary.

A brief moment of delirium in the course of a fever is certainly nothing extraordinary, but for this man to take a cold

bath in October, then to enter his jewelry shop wrapped in a
sheet like a cloak, with his head circled by a handkerchief
like a crown, raving of his coming glories, is to display the
delusions of grandeur that are the beginnings of madness.

As for the terrible scene of January 1868, to which the defense refers simply as "the scene at the hearth," or "the scene
of which the Court has heard," it came only a few months
later; and although the defense does not wish it to be related
to the first scene, dismissing it instead as an accidental folly,
Dr. Pasquier has spoken the truth: it is unmistakably
madness.

It is after such shocks as these that we find those resurrec-
tions so brilliantly described by Maître Carel? Alas, we know
all too well what happens to our poor human intelligence
when it finds itself stricken, agitated, deflected from its journey toward the supreme goal of our destiny. It is at such
times that families anxiously veil the situation in silence,
ever fearing the worst and expecting new crises. After October 1867 Antonio's mother lived in such a state of apprehen-
sion.

The death of Mme Mellerio, and the reproaches of his family and his religion, would not have led him to burn his
hands to the wrists had he not already been prone to insanity.
Alas, we have all endured such cruel bereavements, we have
all experienced such sorrows and prostrations. But in Antonio's case, his weakened mind gave way to frenzy and madness. Is there anything in the annals of lunacy more horrible
than the spectacle of this man, not brought to his senses by
his pain, chanting, like the Indian, his hymn of death?

If one looks further into the future, one sees in Antonio's
poor head the soul straining more and more to break her
worldly ties, wandering through many crooked paths and
finally attempting to mount toward God by means of a violent shock: suicide.

The details of the account given in a regional newspaper
were not invented by its editor. As a retailer of local gossip
[des cancans de la contrée], this newspaper published the interpretation widely prevalent throughout the area. The defense has dared to allege that this account was dictated to the
newspaper by the heirs. This is an outrageous suggestion,

which the speaker repudiates, both on his own behalf and on that of his clients. Tailleville had attracted public attention. The eccentric and mutilated master, the mysterious mistress, so grotesquely draped in piety, the violent death—all provoked comment. That is the source of both the public scandal and the account in the newspaper.

Considering these three periods (October 1867; January 1868; April 1870), and considering the general pattern of behavior that the plaintiffs have cited, they are fully justified in their request for a commission of inquiry to clarify the matter.

The affidavit of Dr. Pasquier, the family physician, has been submitted in evidence. One party of defendents rejects it, the other has chosen to ignore it.

They have tried to make Dr. Pasquier seem to contradict himself. Like many doctors, he was habitually pragmatic; when he saw at Tailleville a woman who nursed his patient, he did not bother himself with the legitimacy of her presence, he complimented her on her solicitude. But when he was required to define the role of Mme Debacker in a sworn affidavit, he told the truth about her as he did about everything else. If he were alive today, he would not retract a single word.

The family have also had used against them both their occasional compliments to Mme Debacker and their avoidance of Antonio. In every family at the beginning of an unsavory situation like that at Tailleville, first the relatives complain and absent themselves, and then they do drift back a little bit—they correspond, for business matters, or for one reason or another, but usually they let it go at that, pretending to accept invitations and then always finding some excuse not to follow through; they are after all husbands and fathers, and they do not wish to involve their families too deeply in certain sorts of intimate relationships. Mme Debacker was living with Antonio, and if she sent her compliments, they were politely returned, for his sake. That is all.

The plaintiffs have not hesitated to produce before this Court the letter of Jousse, knowing full well that they would thus be unable to summon this witness in person in a subsequent commission of inquiry, but they wished to give an ex-

ample of how useful such a commission would be in leading
to important revelations by other witnesses. Jousse's testimony has been impugned. But what motive would he possibly
have in offering it to the Court? The Mellerios are above the
suspicion of suborning witnesses. If one of the defense attorneys has spoken so eloquently in praise of his clients' honor,
he will permit the speaker to take his own clients for men of
integrity. Inquiries have been made about Jousse, who is far
from being the mere bohemian he has been alleged to be, and
they have proved to be satisfactory. This man lived for a short
while in the very midst of Antonio's ravings and the violence
of the irregular household at Tailleville. He exposes them
with an absolute adherence to the truth.

Mme Agnel, one of the plaintiffs in the case, has seen this
spectacle at first hand, and she took careful note of it. She
knows what to think. At her arrival Antonio announced sol-
emnly that the empress had come to see him, and that she
was invisible to everyone except himself and the prefect.

(Glances were turned toward M. Ferrand, who was attend-
ing the session, and who indeed is the current Prefect of Calvados, but he did not hold that office at the time to which the
speaker alludes.)

Paul, the son of Mme Agnel, suffered an attack of sun-
stroke, and fell seriously ill; Mme Debacker helped nurse
him. Naturally his mother thanked her. According to Mme
Agnel, the young Paul began to find Antonio's religious
frenzy contagious, and he would soon have caught the delirium if they had not left Tailleville.

Mme Debacker herself realized that Antonio was eccentric.
The document in which she admits this was drafted by
Maître Hébert, and no one then took exception to its wording. If this wording had been only the family's view of the
matter, Maître Hébert would have included an indication of
dissent, at least by adding some such phrase as, "Although
Mme Debacker asserts the contrary." Such contradictory
views, as yet unreconciled, are found in all such documents
of this sort, before a compromise wording has been reached.
They are not found here because there was no dissent, for
Mme Debacker, like the heirs and implicitly like Maître Hébert, recognized that in fact Antonio had been eccentric.

The relationships Antonio pretended to have with the angels, his strange ablutions—all these things are not instances of some slight mental disorder; the pressure brought to bear on him was not some slight undue influence. It was considerable insanity; it was considerable undue influence. And if, besides the presumptions inherent in the documents presented before this Court, these facts are confirmed by a commission of inquiry, the suit will be won. Thus, such a commission is necessary.

Argument upon argument has been piled up. The heirs have been asked: how could you have done business with a madman? But did they not appoint a guardian for the entailed estate? The proposed declaration of incompetency has been discussed—but it was the family who did not wish that! Or the law of 1838—but the family had always recoiled from such an extremity; it would have been a terrible injustice to Antonio!

The *de cuius* has been described as actively engaged in his business affairs—but of this activity the inventory does not reveal a single trace—it contains no receipts, or even any bills for household expenses. The reason for this is that Antonio was not in charge of, nor did he administer, anything; everything was done by Mme Debacker. She even left him without pocket money. And if there were account books or financial documents, it was she who controlled them and probably included them in the famous "wastepaper."

Except for the letter from Maître Prevost and Antonio's reply (whose absence from the inventory Maître Pilet des Jardins [Mme Debacker's attorney] explains by their having been sent to the family lawyers in Paris before Antonio's death), no solution has been given to this problem of "wastepaper."

Turning to the period preceding that of the last testament [October 1869], the previous testament [June 1869] had been entirely in order, as far as Mme Debacker was concerned, but it was thought necessary to formalize the provisions dealing with charity. Why, we are asked, should Mme Debacker have cared if that portion were in order? Would not the contrary have been more in her interest, since this last testament took from her a significant share of the estate while the previous one, making her sole beneficiary, was entirely valid? But we ought not to forget that Mme Debacker would have been anxious to have a testament that did not betray the least trace of insanity in any of its sections. Maître Hébert contented himself with providing a model. Why did he not think he should himself draw up an incontestable testament? The lawyer in Paris, Maître Prevost, was more forthright: he said clearly what the family's rights were and what nevertheless Antonio might do for the charitable foundation and for Mme Debacker. If only every notary and lawyer always gave such sound advice!

In the end Antonio decided against his family, though in his earlier testaments, left to his own devices, he had not forgotten them. In his reply to Maître Prevost, "I am acting on my own," he really meant, "I am not alone," nor do his praises of Anna fool anyone—Anna was dictating the letter. Now, this answer from Antonio to Maître Prevost is apparently very damaging to the plaintiffs, because it seems to show a fixed resolve. But in explaining how this piece of "wastepaper" got to Paris, the defendants have revealed that it was previously kept for a time by Mme Debacker. Now, since Mme Debacker had the key to the mailbox, she would have received Maître Prevost's letter from the mailman; and since she also had the keeping of it, together with the reply that Antonio wrote on the back of the page, it is certainly plausible that she did not relinquish it while Antonio was writing that reply.

It was also she who had possession of the last testament, the product of this *ménage*. This last testament was never properly filed.

Antonio may have performed some sensible acts, but if a man is mad, occasional sensible acts do not rule out insanity, particularly where an *idée fixe* is concerned—such as, in this case, the question of legacies. The essential condition of the human soul is unity; when this unity is shattered, the result is necessarily insanity.

As for undue influence, Maître Allou declared plainly [printed in the newspaper in large type, widely spaced]:

"It never crossed my mind to cast any such aspersions on the Convent. My grammatical negative was misinterpreted.

When I said that, as far as they were concerned, there had been no *shameless undue influence,* I never meant that there had been *some other kind*; I was thus acknowledging that *as far as they were concerned there had been none of the shamelessness of undue influence.* In a word, I had not in the slightest degree intended nor wished to accuse the Convent. I accordingly absolve it completely from any charge of undue influence."

Maître Allou is saddened to find in the dossier a letter from the priest at Garges (near Paris) containing an enormous amount of advice about the testament. He would also have preferred to see, from the pens of various ecclesiastics appealing to the charity of Mellerio and Mme Debacker, expressions a little less obsequious.

(Some persons, at the back of the chamber, felt it necessary to emphasize this sentiment with a murmur of approval.)

Maître Allou, who never lent himself to the sensationalism some people have hoped to find in this case, added immediately:

"The murmurs that I hear seem (as in the case of Monday's laughter) to pervert my meaning. I only regretted encountering expressions that perhaps erred from an excess of zeal. That is all. But let it be well understood that I did not mean to ascribe guilt to any person or to any intention, and there I limit the reflections that I think it advisable to make on this subject."

Mme Debacker exerted undue influence over Antonio—that charge is all the case requires. She forcibly carried him off after the death of his mother. No one, neither Dr. Pasquier nor Morel, gave her news of him. They had been charged with making her believe that Antonio was in Italy, and with negotiating with her the question of the separation. The alleged sending of the drawing [of cupids] is a pure fiction. This drawing is dated 18 March, which is the date of its execution and not of its alleged sending. It shows cupids drawn by horses, and is more probably some kind of copy of a cameo from a museum at Naples than an appeal for a new life of rehabilitation *à deux.* Mme Debacker no doubt found it at the château.

Morel is at hand to testify that he was never asked to take

her this drawing. Morel is at hand to testify to her cry, on recovering Antonio, "I have him!"—and then we shall learn if that cry was an expression of tenderness or of undue influence.

Jousse is at hand to testify that one day in speaking of Antonio Mme Debacker remarked that religion was the only hold she had on him. And she may be seen encouraging him in religious mania and exploiting every possible manifestation of a deranged mysticism.

With the increase of Antonio's generosity may be seen the intensification of Mme Debacker's maneuvering.

She has used the name of a Convent of holy maidens, the name of a Convent devoted to charity, to gain control over Antonio for her own profit and to disguise and protect the testament by the inclusion of respectable legatees who thus would also find themselves interested parties.

It has been asserted, on behalf of Mme Debacker, that the gift of an annual income of 12,000 francs, which set her free at once whereas a legacy would have held her to the end, was an act of delicacy on Antonio's part as well as a method of testing her affections, and that Mme Debacker demonstrated the sincerity of her affection for Antonio by remaining with him. But it should not be forgotten that the endowment of an income did not nullify the testament, and that the immediate acquisition of the one gift need not have prevented Mme Debacker from continuing her maneuvers to assure herself of the other. [This apparently telling point neglects to mention that the annuity was given to Mme Debacker *in lieu of* previous legacies (p. 98).]

Le sieur Debacker was necessarily a party to this gift of an income [under French law married women may not participate in legal affairs without the authorization of their husbands]; the husband, the wife, and the lover were all involved together. Such behavior is truly vile.

The plaintiffs persist in urging a commission of inquiry. It has been called an extreme expedient. Any litigant who seeks the truth in such a commission sees no reason to call it that; any who fears it can imagine nothing worse. It is the old story, found in every dispute. But nevertheless, a commission of inquiry is a legitimate legal procedure often necessary for discovering the truth.

On the subject of this affair, Maître Allou has heard, far and wide, totally discrepant versions and totally contradictory opinions. They can only be sorted out fairly by a commission of inquiry.

The results of the undue influence successfully practiced even for a moment by Mme Debacker, and of the unsoundness of mind that led a man to impoverish his own family for the sake of a mistress and a religious community, ought not to be allowed to stand.

Antonio's family have come before the bar of justice because they have confidence that the Court will so decide.

Maître Pilet des Jardins declared himself satisfied with the way the case had developed [thereby waiving his right to a turn at rebuttal].

The abundance of material in this case obliges us to defer Maître Carel's reply to the next issue.

(To be continued.)

[*L'Ordre et la Liberté*, Monday-Tuesday, 24–25 June 1872]

Session of 19 June 1872

(Conclusion)

The counsel for the Convent has the floor.

"What I most appreciate," says Maître Carel, "is not the praise by which the distinguished attorney whom we have just heard encourages my meager talents; what flatters me most, because it represents the major triumph of the interests confided to me, what I find most gratifying, is the free and entire dismissal of all charges of undue influence against the Convent of la Charité des Orphelines de Marie de la Délivrande.

"This Convent, which was purported to have been the accomplice in a secretly hatched plot, this Convent, which was to have been made the subject of scandal, has emerged spotless from the toils of this dispute. The forces of truth have repulsed an attempted assault, and instead of a Convent conniving to practice undue influence, we have simply a charitable foundation learning after the death of a testator that it has received a legacy and taking upon itself the duty of claiming that legacy in the name of the poor.

"This time, I trust, we do not have a rhetorical concession that I am now 'abusing,' but a public acknowledgment, made, Your Honors, before your Court."

Maître Carel has little to add, but there do remain a few observations he would like to make.

On the subject of the letter from the priest at Garges, that priest is not at hand to testify, nor is it the speaker's duty to defend him. But, in any case, the matter merely concerns a letter, written by an ecclesiastic living near Paris, that seems to be a reply to a request for advice concerning the legal formalities of a charitable legacy, but that in no way may be said to contain even the least improper insinuation.

Maître Allou has regretted "certain obsequious phrases" employed by some priests in dealing with Antonio and Mme Debacker while asking their help on behalf of the poor. But in fact such obsequiousness ought rather to be praised than blamed, because to humble oneself in this way, holding out one's hand in supplication to relieve the misery of others, is a truly beautiful act. When Christian charity knocks at the doors of the rich, it must often abase itself and beg. Such humility is a virtue of which not everyone is capable.

It has been asserted that many of the plaintiffs' arguments have prudently been left unanswered. But the speaker has disregarded nothing. Antonio had two fits, which have been the subject of ample discussion. There is no need to return to them again. As far as the Convent's suit is concerned, the important fact is that Antonio did recover his health: that is the crux of the case. [Maître Carel, as counsel for the convent, is naturally concerned to protect only its interests, whatever may happen with respect to Mme Debacker. Thus, since all charges of undue influence against the convent have just been dropped, the allegations of Mellerio's unsoundness of mind are all that remain to threaten the convent's reception of its portion of the legacy.]

When madness overwhelms a personality as exuberant as Antonio's, it reveals itself in symptoms of insanity that, after their first appearance, persist and multiply. In his case there was first an attack of fever, then a terrible scene after which, had his mind really succumbed to madness, would have followed other obvious symptoms of disorder. But that is not what we see here at all. His prompt recovery may be traced, step by step, without the slightest evidence of unsoundness of mind.

The effort to link the alleged suicide to these two episodes is hopeless. Moreover, if this suicide is nothing more than a simple accident, the argument collapses entirely—and who would dare swear before God that it was a suicide? And anyway, even if it is asserted tht he did suffer a third attack on that fatal day, had not Antonio in the meantime enjoyed the free exercise of his mental faculties, particularly at the time of drawing up the testament? And what more is needed?

In such situations as this, which may have occurred before, and indeed certainly have occurred before, legal precedent may be legitimately invoked. Yet you [the plaintiffs] reject it disdainfully, you spurn all previous judgments, you tell the Court that it alone is sovereign. But no, the Court is not sovereign: it is subject both to the law and to the authority of legal precedent.

In answer to the heaps of documents introduced by the defense to demonstrate Antonio's perfect soundness of mind, in his personal relations, in his acts of charity, and in his business dealings, the plaintiffs cite the inventory's lack of records of household expenses. They are thus reduced to searching in this absence of bills from the laundress and the cook for proof as to whether or not the master of Tailleville was insane. The answer will be found in the decidedly more significant documents introduced before the Court.

The indivisibility of the human mind has been invoked. And properly so. "Well, then!" cries the speaker. "Let the documents be read, of every sort and from every period after the scene at the fireplace; if, in *this* commission of inquiry— the most intimate possible and the only true such inquiry— any gap in Antonio's sanity is to be found, then what I am claiming is indeed rash, our case perhaps lost. But we fear nothing, for there you will find the man risen as from the dead.

"If the shock was terrific, the recovery was magnificent: both mind and health were reborn, stronger than ever. It is a miracle that dazzles the eye: we see here today, in all its splendor, the truth, which tomorrow may be sadly distorted by the bizarre hazards of a commission of inquiry."

Then Maître Carel took up the Pasquier affidavit. The doctor never saw Antonio at all during the long period at the château. Even when psychologists have followed closely the entire course of a mental illness, they still hesitate to deny the existence of any occasional glimmer of rationality; and yet here we have a person who did not witness the marvelous recovery, who did not see the suicide—and who still presumes to offer testimony tracing links between far distant events. If the plaintiffs have in reserve any more of such witnesses who have seen nothing, their desire for a commission of inquiry is understandable. Faced with the information that this current legal process has brought to light, there is no doubt that Dr. Pasquier, were he still alive, would have the integrity to withdraw his attestations.

As for Mme Agnel and her recollections of the sayings and doings at Tailleville, she is well aware what slight value such testimony has, coming from an interested party. But she has in her possession evidence that is much more eloquent: she has all the correspondence between her and Antonio, and had there been a single trace of madness in a single one of those letters, that letter would long since have appeared before this Court.

As for the letter from Jousse, this man is one of those witnesses who does not have to be suborned—he volunteers! In the speaker's earlier remarks, he never wished to imply that the plaintiffs had suborned Jousse, he meant to say that Jousse had misled them. No one could have confidence in this *ex post facto* letter, these belated recriminations that could never invalidate Antonio's testament.

The counsel for the Convent thus claims that he has not left anything unanswered. If he has admittedly neglected details irrelevant to the case, he has omitted nothing relevant. The facts and arguments pertaining to the case have been dealt with, and on them alone will the Court fix its attention.

"On the day," said Maître Carel to the plaintiffs, "on the day that you bought the Mellerio business from Antonio, you deprived yourselves of the right to cast suspicion on his sanity. One cousin, Antoine, assessed the value of the business, and another, Joseph, took title to it. The goodwill was declared to be worth only 10,000 francs; all the rest of the price—a considerable sum—was that of the jewelry and the unset stones. Now, Joseph was the appraiser. Within a family, among men of honor, such arrangements may be made with propriety. But take care! Otherwise, you will be presenting yourself as experts dealing in your own field with a man who would not have had the competence to bestow his confidence on you, who would not have known how to defend his own interests—in a word, who would have been a man whom you knew to be of unsound mind!

"You have found him competent to entrust you with recovering sizable debts owed to him; you have found him competent to keep at his disposal, after the establishment of the estate in joint-possession, half of that valuable patrimony; you have found him competent to manage his own affairs, because you have dealt with him in matters both large and small. Once more, take care lest you attack him! Take good care, because you would be attacking yourselves! But no, it is not possible that you can have so blatantly violated the code of honor. You are actually here to testify that Antonio really was of sound mind. You yourselves are his best witnesses!"

So the speaker persists in asserting that Antonio was of sound mind, that the long residence at Tailleville was restorative, and that, particularly with reference to the time when the testament was drawn up, all the evidence proves that he was in full and free possession of his mental faculties. And that is the question to be decided.

The Convent cannot be accused of undue influence, the testament is therefore valid, and the Court, with the ample evidence already available to it, will uphold it.

The Court is adjourned until Wednesday [one week later], when it will hear the opinion of the Public Prosecutor.

[Also from *L'Ordre et la Liberté*,
Monday–Tuesday, 24–25 June 1872]

Last week, the name of Mellerio rang elsewhere than in the Hall of Justice at Caen. The Civil Court of the Seine (First Chamber) has just ordered the former Queen Isabelle [of Spain] to pay 146,750 francs to M. Mellerio, with interest and costs, in payment for several pieces of jewelry.

The matter concerned jewelry delivered to Isabelle on the occasion of the marriage of her daughter, Princess de Girgenti. [For fuller details on this case, see the Appendix.]

[*L'Ordre et la Liberté*, Thursday, 4 July 1872]

In today's session [Wednesday, 3 July], M. Cosnards-Desclozets, the Public Prosecutor [on the function of this official, see pp. 21–22, and below], gave his opinion rejecting the request for a commission of inquiry, and thus upheld the validity of the acts in question.

[*L'Ordre et la Liberté*, Saturday, 6 July 1872]

Session of Wednesday, 3 July 1872

The next session of this case, which was to have taken place on 26 June, was postponed until today for the speech of the Public Prosecutor.

If it was not without reluctance that we undertook the task of summarizing the pleadings of the attorneys, how much more do we mistrust our talents as we approach the address of the Public Prosecutor. However, we must finish what we have begun. We will do so with all possible care and fidelity, and we are prepared to correct any error that may have slipped into our notes and from there onto our penpoint.

M. Cosnards-Desclozets, chief of the judicial magistrates, has the floor.

The task of the Public Prosecutor is twofold: first, to make a summary of the arguments, without allowing himself to be swayed by the brilliant and dramatic language in which they are clothed, and then to extract from these speeches and from the documentary evidence of the case the legal grounds on which it is to be decided.

This latter duty has four essential parts:
1) To study in the pleadings the issues that were prominent in debate.
2) To study the documents submitted in evidence.
3) To review the cited precedents of nullification.
4) To determine the propriety of ordering a commission of inquiry.

In 1870 Mme Debacker petitioned for a writ of possession entitling her to the legacy made to her by the holographic testament of Antonio Mellerio, dated 21 October 1869, and reading as follows:

"This is my testament.

"I hereby name Mme Debacker, née Anna Trayer, my sole beneficiary, with the single exception of the following bequest:

"I give and bequeath to the Convent of la Charité des Orphelines de la Délivrande my property at Tailleville, that is, all the real estate that I possess in the townships of Tailleville, Bernières, Langrune, and Bény, together with the sum of two hundred thousand francs from the remainder of my estate; but the Convent of the Orphelines de la Charité [*sic*] de la Délivrande is not to enter into possession of the said legacy until the death of Mme Debacker, who will have the usufruct of it during her lifetime. All transfer fees and other expenses connected with the execution of this testament are to be paid by my sole beneficiary.

"Tailleville, this 21st day of October, 1869.

"Signed: A. Mellerio."

The response to this petition was a suit for nullification. The natural heirs of Antonio Mellerio sued for the annulment, not only of this testament, but of all gifts, whether testamentary or *inter vivos*, or whatever, made by Antonio. As grounds for nullification they cited unsoundness of mind, deprivation of liberty, undue influence, and violence. They listed numerous facts to be demonstrated bearing on their allegations. These documents and events were to be their supporting evidence.

Their suit was for nullification *de plano*. The offers of testimonial proof were subsidiary.

The Convent necessarily found itself involved in the case, and in the arguments it took the unequivocal position we have heard.

What are these gifts whose validity is at issue?

1) Antonio Mellerio, who died in 1870, had known Mme Debacker since 1853. On 25 February 1865, that is, after 12 years, he bequeathed her 120,000 francs of his own inheritance from his father's death in 1860.

2) On 7 January 1868, after the scene by the deathbed, he increased this legacy to 150,000 francs and bequeathed to his family the remainder of his estate.

3) On 4 June of the same year, he left Mme Debacker half of his estate.

These testaments are holographs. They were sealed and filed, each in turn, with Maître Hébert, a notary at Douvres, who left on record that he had seen Antonio write the last one with his mouth.

4) On 17 September 1868, before the same notary, Antonio settled on Mme Debacker an annuity of 12,000 francs, in lieu of his earlier legacies.

5) On 18 June 1869 he made a new holographic testament in which he named Mme Debacker his sole legatee and charged her with executing a charitable legacy. Here are the terms of this document:

"Tailleville, 18 June 1869.

"To my testament on file with Maître Hébert, I hereby add that I name Mme Debacker my sole legatee. I wish that after her death Tailleville be converted into an alms-house or a hospital for crippled paupers, and that it bear the name, carved in the pediment, of St. Joseph's Asylum.

"All Tailleville's income, without exception, is to become the property of St. Joseph's Asylum for the sick. I wish also that the park remain as it is, in the care of M. Legendre or his descendants, likewise for Richer.

"Signed: Antonio Mellerio."

M. Legendre was his private secretary, and Richer his gardener.

Antonio filed this testament, sealed like the others, with Maître Hébert; but—and this fact is worth noting—he asked for the earlier testaments in order to reread them before filing this one.

6) Finally, on 21 October 1869, he wrote the bequests whose text has been given above. These were the last. This testament was not filed; it was produced by Mme Debacker.

If these acts are scrutinized with regard both to their form and to their intention, what is found?

Not one word of the arguments criticizes their form; indeed, that is quite unassailable.

Of their intention, what can be concluded, other than Mellerio's persistent intention to divide his estate into two parts?

During his mother's lifetime, Mme Debacker's portion of
Antonio's estate was already 120,000 francs. After the shock
of Mme Mellerio's death, he increased that portion. Then, as
soon as he controlled his entire estate, he gave her half. Previously he had taken cognizance of the family; this time he
was silent on that score. Then came a gift *inter vivos* to re-
confirm his intentions toward Mme Debacker. A new testament again assigned her a share, as the division of the estate
reappears with the entry of the poor. The question of the
legal phrasing of this bequest is not particularly relevant—
the testator's intention is clear. And finally the division of
the estate returns once more, asserting itself in proper form,
in the last testament, together with the ever persistent intention with regard to Mme Debacker.

Preconceived notions aside, these acts, formally irreproachable, display unmistakably the growth and persistent progression of Antonio's intentions regarding the double goal
he wished to attain.

Having clarified the issues of the case, and examined the
documents on which the debate was based, we now turn to
the alleged grounds for nullification.

Now, in this debate there was no question of law, only of
fact [in marked contrast to the second appeal, in 1874, which
bore heavily on differing interpretations of various articles
in the Civil Code and the Code of Civil Procedure—see chapter 6]. Nevertheless, there do exist certain elementary rules
that are always useful to keep in mind, and certain legal def-
initions that figure prominently in the foreground.

The first ground for contesting Antonio's generosity was
unsoundness of mind. Article 901 of the Civil Code justly
requires that a man who makes a gift, whether *inter vivos* or
by testament, be of sound mind. Soundness of mind—need it
be defined?—means that the testator has: 1) intelligence. He
understands his act and its implications. 2) intention. He
wishes his intentions to be respected and executed. In a word,
he must both understand and intend. The law has set rigorous standards for these conditions, but it also wishes that the
testator who has understood and who has intended be

obeyed. *Dicat testator et erit lex!* according to Roman law.
[Let the testator's wish be law.]

Now, it is understood that if madness is intermittent, if it
yields for a moment to glimmers of understanding, during
which the testator is really *sui compos*, then that instant is
sufficient for the act which he then performs to be unassailable.

What proof then should the Mellerio heirs submit in alleging Antonio's unsoundness of mind as grounds of nullification? They should offer to prove that this unsoundness of
mind was continuous, and that there was either lunacy or
idiocy. We shall see if these charges are successfully proven
by the allegations they have listed.

Likewise, in order to demonstrate undue influence, it is
necessary to show that the testator's intention was altered,
that he was entrapped by fraudulent maneuvers, that another's intention thus was substituted for his own, and that finally he was forced by these measures to make arrangements
other than he would have done through his own free will.

These are the fundamental principles of the case.

Therefore, it is necessary to inquire into the origins of Antonio's mental derangement, to investigate his condition,
and to discover if the alleged facts make it doubtful that he
was of sound mind and that his intention was free.

The Mellerio heirs have asserted that a mental weakness
was the fatal cause of Antonio's falling prey to a madness
that made him helpless to resist first his sensual passions and
then his religious obsessions, holding him in its power and
delivering him up without defense to undue influence, suggestion, and all sorts of mental violence.

With the help of letters going back twenty years, very different portraits have been painted of Antonio. On one side of
the court, he has been depicted as a young man of the highest
intelligence and education, but also lavish, given to undisci-
plined behavior from the age of seventeen, gradually neglect-
ing his work for gambling and orgies, and by the age of
twenty-five exhausted, burnt-out by the fever of passion. On
the other side, in contrast, the portrait changes: there he is a
brilliant and charming personality, enjoying, it is true, fac-
ile amorous successes but never indulging in anything other

than the thoughtless follies that were considered mere pec-
cadillos in Parisian high society, while continuing to instruct his brother in morality, accusing himself in those letters of purely imaginary moral lapses, enjoying his work,
cherishing his parents, concentrating on business, and so
forth.

Both accounts exaggerate. Mellerio was actually neither so
entirely virtuous nor so entirely wicked. As Maître Allou put
it so well, his mind was so very impressionable that it knew
no balance. By the side of the sweetest expressions of family
feeling may be found traces of the wildest profligacy: he is
truly a man with two faces.

The true implications of his correspondence have not yet
been explored as thoroughly as they deserve, however remote
their bearing on the case may be. They provide, alas, an example of youth thrown into the swirl of Parisian society,
lacking principle, lacking convictions, and seeking in dissipation and debauchery a life of pleasure. Thousands of
times, episodes from such deplorable lives have unfolded in
courtrooms. But are they ever taken as displaying an absence
of will? Never.

Mellerio, like the others, had one passion above all: vanity.
A woman whom he could not possess drove him not to despair but to anger. In his triumphs he was never seen to sur-
render; he gave his heart to none of them. He took what he
wanted from each: he liked to be seen driving with one; he
would take tea in the luxurious apartment of another; he
would appear at the theater with a third. He dominated them
all, he yielded to none. His lavishness was calculated—he
knew what they all cost. At the gambling table he kept track
of his losses and stopped where he meant to. In all his behavior there blazed a masterful will that nothing could control.
Adroit and impressionable indeed, as much as you like, but
even in this unhealthy *milieu* his will was sovereign; he always kept his self-control completely intact.

Such was the origin of Antonio's liaison with Mme Debacker, a liaison that was destined to last all his life. We will
soon see if Mme Debacker, having conquered his heart, made
off with Antonio's willpower as well.

It is not part of the Public Prosecutor's duty to go into

Mme Debacker's early history. In a civil case like this, the moral aspects of the affair are not at issue. But from a point of view above and beyond his legal role in this particular case, it is clearly his duty to censure behavior as illicit as it is scandalous.

In the interpretation [of the last few years of Antonio's life] offered by the Mellerio heirs, there figure certain crucial events.

Among these are the extravagant expenses involved in the decoration of Tailleville after the death of Antonio's father, a trip to Paris on that account, and a subsequent violent scene with his mother. Now, these assertions are at least dubious, because in the letters of Mme Mellerio there cannot be found one single reproach. Only once she quietly gave him to understand that if he had not spent so much it would have been possible to buy some property that one of their friends was selling.

Then there was the attack of fever after the cold bath of October 1867, which has not gone undiscussed. Then the terrible scene at the fireplace, in January 1868, which was an act of religious frenzy, a real attack of madness that lasted for several weeks. Finally, the death, in April 1870.

Was the death voluntary or accidental? Both hypotheses are possible, but there is not a single adequate reason for resorting to hypothesis. Throughout the many letters, of which Antonio kept copies, as if in foreknowledge that they would be needed to settle this dispute, his affection for Mme Debacker appears full and enduring. His happiness is complete; he seems to know neither annoyance nor ennui. Well, if one really sympathizes with a soul so utterly content, clinging so dearly to life, how can suicide be seen as a possibility? [*Red Cotton Night-Cap Country* might well be considered a 4,000-line answer to this single question.] Suicide is at least unlikely, very unlikely. The circumstances of the site, the maimed condition of the man, the possibility of vertigo—all combined to make an accident extremely plausible. Though indeed, considering all the possibilities, it would be foolhardy to claim certain knowledge one way or the other.

At the time of the scenes of October 1867 [the bath] and January 1868 [the mutilation], the state of insanity seems to have been constant. But was there recovery or was there not? What was Antonio's mental condition apart from this period?

What is required for the plaintiffs' case is not proof of just a little or even a great deal of unsoundness of mind, nor proof of just a little or even a great deal of undue influence; what is required is a full series of facts, established as evidence in a court of law, that are relevant to the disputed acts and that make it impossible to suppose that for even one moment while he was performing those acts Antonio had full use of his mental powers—his intelligence and his will.

The Public Prosecutor then reviewed the plaintiffs' list of allegations.

The first eight allegations deal with the origins of the liaison between Antonio and Mme Debacker; there is nothing of special interest to be found there, except for the sea [le vague] of letters. Numbers 9 and 10 concern the attack of October 1867, which has been thoroughly gone into. The following series [nos. 11–26] involves the scenes of January 1868, by the bed of Mme Mellerio, at the fireplace, and at the cemetery of Garges, after which Antonio fell prey to mysterious fears and undertook the break with Mme Debacker. Numbers 27 and 28 recount her pursuit of Antonio and their new life together.

Then came the religious rites [no. 31], the outlandish exaggerations, the rejected request for a chaplain [no. 35], the letters from the so-called Father Joseph, and so on [nos. 41–42, 50], the purchase of religious objects [no. 37], the ceremonies of thanksgiving in the middle of the road [no. 39], the personal ablutions [no. 54], the servants required to do likewise to imitate the celestial spirits [no. 55], the burial of the meat [nos. 56–57]—followed by general assertions implying the complete annihilation of his intelligence [no. 58], the challenges to a duel over a rabbit [no. 59], and finally the public gossip about madness and suicide [nos. 61–63].

A second document submits further allegations in evidence: terrors, visions; [In the pleadings as filed in the court records, the allegations mentioned here as being listed in a "second document" were interspersed among the other allegations, as may be seen from the gaps in the sequence of the bracketed numbers. It seems plausible to infer from the contents of these added allegations that this "second document" must be the letter from the ungrateful Jousse.] Antonio believed he saw the devil in the billiard room [no. 42]; his mother's spirit appeared to him [no. 43]; he had violent quarrels with Mme Debacker, even chasing her from the dinner table [no. 45]. At night, cries were heard coming from their rooms [no. 47]. He wished to give the church money to avoid damnation [no. 50]; he asked Jousse, his guest for a short while, for the hand of his daughter in order to be rid of Mme Debacker [no. 51].

The Public Prosecutor considers that even if this entire list of allegations were proved to be true, it would be evidence of real (though intermittent) madness, but not at all of continuous insanity.

A single piece of evidence has been brought in at the last minute that does seem to support the family's claim: the affidavit of Dr. Pasquier.

This document has been given an exaggerated importance. To be understood properly, it should be divided into two parts:

In the first part, the doctor attests to the events he has seen, citing Antonio's mental troubles—the frenzies, first of eroticism, and then of religion in 1867 and 1868 at the scenes in Paris and Garges. To give credence to these attestations is already to be generous, because they concern nothing more than superficial observations, without any very close psychological examination or any very thoughtful reflection.

The second part hazards interpretations, at a distance of 60 leagues [150 miles] of events that the doctor had not seen, and concerning which he had had no disinterested evidence whatsoever. By an imaginative set of inferences, he leaped a considerable gap between the death of Antonio—the causes of which he had no certain knowledge of—and the earlier events that he did know about, and he presumed therefrom to draw conclusions. One should not swear to facts other than those that one has personally witnessed. Dr. Pasquier, honorable man that he was, certainly overreached himself here.

(To be continued.)

104

[*L'Ordre et la Liberté*, Sunday, 7 July 1872]

Session of 3 July 1872

(Conclusion)

The counsel for the natural heirs has not claimed that Antonio suffered from either lunacy or idiocy; he has merely argued that there did occur undeniable crises of madness that linked up with each other and made undue influence easier to exert. Consequently, this position abandons absolute lunacy or idiocy, and does not allege continuous madness; these concessions have enormous consequences with regard to the unsoundness of mind they are concerned to prove.

According to the rules of evidence, the task of the heirs is twofold: in their petition for a commission of inquiry, they must bring before the Court pertinent and admissible evidence that can establish either that Antonio suffered from lunacy, an absolute madness, or at least that he was a victim of this insanity, this unsoundness of mind, during the periods in which he performed his various acts of generosity.

Now, since the question of absolute madness was abandoned, it remains unestablished and cannot serve as the basis for ordering a commission of inquiry. And since unsoundness of mind only at the times of the disputed acts did not even figure in the plaintiffs' argument, it need not be considered here. [Here the public prosecutor located the fatal flaw of the heirs' argument concerning Mellerio's unsoundness of mind. The plaintiffs' brief for the 1873 appeal would endeavor to correct this error.]

The conclusion must be drawn that those disputed acts were in fact performed during periods when Antonio enjoyed the full play of his mental powers. The legal presumption is one of soundness of mind.

Therefore, from the point of view of Antonio's mental condition, the claims of the heirs are denied.

And after all, while he was alive, was or was not Mellerio generally considered sane?

There are no relevant facts cited for the period between the attack of October 1867 and that of January 1868. After the crisis that led to the terrifying scene at the fireplace, what did

Morel have to say—Morel, the accountant, the friend, the confidant? He reported that Antonio's mental health was improving even faster than his physical health. Morel is alleged to have muted these bulletins. But has it not been remarked that Antonio's participation in business affairs increased at exactly the same pace as the restoration of mental health documented by the correspondence of this honest witness? This is an important consideration. Moreover, if this correspondence is studied in detail, it may be seen that, far from having been reserved with Maître Hébert, Morel discussed to the point of indiscretion any event that might possibly cast light on Mellerio's recovery.

Moreover, the case is full of facts that make it possible to learn the real mental state of the *de cuius*. Forty-five files of intimate documents of all sorts constitute a series of daguerrotypes of this life in all its phases. Some months after the terrible attack in which he lost his hands, Antonio regained control of his mind and devoted himself to serious financial affairs. There was the liquidation of the jewelry business, concerning which he is seen consulting with that responsible man, Maître Prevost. There was his role in the sale of the stock and goodwill, the appraisal that depended on his acquiescence, the collection of monies owed to him, the arrangements made to settle these accounts, and the delay of payment for ten years, which the family was glad to accept from him. And what sort of person would have conducted negotiations on such important matters with a madman?!

There is also the sale of property at Langrune, at Garges, and so on, whose terms were fully and clearly discussed, particularly in the case of the garden at Garges, for which Antonio eventually obtained from the buyer a price higher than that which was first offered. Later, working with Maître Hébert, he negotiated a loan of 35,000 francs.

This variety of extremely important acts demonstrates that he was perfectly capable of exercising his civil rights. These acts were influenced by no one. Antonio may be seen administering his financial affairs—transferring property, lending money, selling assets—all with intelligence, order, and circumspection.

Consequently, the legal presumption of soundness of mind is impressively confirmed.

The same principles that govern annulment on the grounds of unsoundness of mind govern annulment on the grounds of undue influence. What is required here is a set of fraudulent maneuvers, effectively corrupting the intention of the testator and supplanting it with the intention of another. These maneuvers should be appropriate for the intelligence of the individual against whom they are being directed. If Antonio had remained a victim of those crises that had weakened his mind, certainly the maneuvers should be easier to detect.

Originally, when both legatees were charged with undue influence, two different arguments were used. In the first, the written pleadings alleged an association of persons whom the Public Prosecutor was extremely surprised to see thus allied. At la Délivrande, it was alleged, both religious communities endeavored to establish relations with Antonio and Mme Debacker. (The Public Prosecutor here cited extracts from the Mellerio statement on this subject.)

There was a letter from a priest soliciting an interview for Antonio with the Mother Superior of the Convent, after which, the statements reads, in speaking of Tailleville, "Moreover, it was the Convent of la Délivrande that took the responsibility of finding servants for this household." Certainly, that is an allegation with very serious implications. And then follows a series of three letters from Antonio on this subject.

There are no dates given for these three letters, although, in the opinion of the Public Prosecutor, there should be. The statement of the plaintiffs goes on to say: "Not only did Antonio Mellerio write in the manner we have just indicated, but the Convent responded." Then follows a letter, addressed to Antonio, which also deals with finding a servant and which comes from the Convent de la Vierge Fidèle, but this time with a date, 20 February 1870. And this portion of the statement then concludes, "Mme Debacker had dismissed all the servants whose influence on Antonio interfered with her plans, and she wished to have them replaced by servants selected from the neighboring convent." And finally comes a letter from the priest at Garges, which is apparently an answer to Antonio's request for advice concerning his rights to dispose of his estate.

This sequence is extremely important, because it alleges a fraudulent arrangement between the Convent and Mme Debacker to use the consultation with the priest at Garges for their own ends.

The relevant supporting evidence has been reviewed. This includes Mme Debacker's pursuit of Antonio to the Champs-Elysées to seize him after the death of his mother, his capture, followed by the flight to the rue Miromesnil, Mme Debacker's cry of triumph, the return to Tailleville, Antonio's religious obsessions, his hallucinations, the almost daily contact with the Monastery of the Missionary Fathers, and the Convent of the Orphans (otherwise known as la Vierge-Fidèle), the resulting influence over Antonio achieved with the help of Mme Debacker, the selection of servants by the Convent, Antonio's request for a chaplain, the consultation with the priest at Garges, and so on.

In all this material two points should be observed. The thrust of this evidence is to associate the religious orders with Mme Debacker, and also to impute the active role in this intrigue to the religious orders. Hardly any acts are charged against Mme Debacker—only the pursuit in the Champs-Elysées, the capture of Antonio, and the famous "I have him!" If all the rest of this evidence is examined, she is nowhere to be found, except in the common charge that deals with the dismissal of the servants.

In a second set of charges are brought forward the testimony of Jousse, then that of Father Joseph, who is an ecclesiastic introduced without any mention of who he is or where he comes from. Then comes Mme Debacker, armed and dangerous, in a veritable reign of terror, with several outbursts involving servants, and so on.

In this way the plaintiffs have sought to establish between the Convent and Mme Debacker a fraudulent relationship of deplorable complicity. They did not pause before the difficulties inherent in alleging a conspiracy, amounting to undue influence, involving pious ladies who could neither

leave their cloister nor allow it to be entered. Such a procedure on the part of the Mellerio heirs can only be described as
reckless frivolity [*une légèreté bien imprudente*].

It is not the task of the Public Prosecutor to defend all
convents in general. But it is insolent [*téméraire*] to bring
such wild charges into court, because such actions will close
the doors of the Court to respectable persons who will hesitate to come to be treated in such a fashion, since, no matter
how vindicated they may finally be, some portion of their
reputation must inevitably be lost.

It is insolent to offer as evidence of such collusion the letter
of 27 February 1870, as was done, since it is later by several
months than the last testament; it is insolent to adduce as
relevant the letter from Garges, which is concerned only with
general conclusions arrived at from a distance of over 60
leagues away, and which does not contain a single allusion
to the Convent; and finally, it is insolent to offer as important evidence letters for which no dates are given. Through
such memorandums, scattered as they may be over several
previous months, it is possible to lay a plausible foundation
for deceptive allegations. Nowadays, when religious communities are so frequently coming under attack, it becomes
the duty of the Public Prosecutor to protest against such
methods.

In the trial itself things were different. There the Public
Prosecutor compliments the attorney for the Mellerio heirs
on his fairness. In his verbal pleadings he simply reproached
the Convent for the cautiousness of its discretion. In his rebuttal he was even plainer, acknowledging that there had
been no trace of undue influence on the part of the Convent.
He remained content with criticizing certain phrases stem-
ming from an excess of zeal. The only role of the Convent
was then said to be that of serving as a cloak with which Mme
Debacker sought to cover herself, or, in the words of one of
the speakers, as a "halo" with which Mme Debacker sought
to protect from attack acts of generosity of which she herself
was the beneficiary.

But even if charges of undue influence against the Convent are dismissed, there nevertheless still remain against
Mme Debacker charges not only of undue influence but of

109

violence as well. Concern for the truth has obliged the Public Prosecutor to dwell at some length on the subject of the Convent. However, the task of examining the role of Mme Debacker has thereby been made easier.

The method of the Public Prosecutor will be the process of elimination.

Undue influence is displayed in objective events. There are certain familiar and almost classical techniques, which create a vacuum around the testator, driving off his friends and relatives, and hemming him in so as to leave him susceptible to domination. Did such events occur at Tailleville? Undeniably, there did exist a sort of isolation from friends and family, but it was an isolation created by those who, although repeatedly invited and even begged to visit, decided not to. Granted, it was Antonio's peculiar situation that kept them away, but the decision to remain absent was theirs alone. Thus, there is no proof of undue influence to be found in this line of approach.

There is also the question of sequestration—but every day Antonio went out, hunted, and moved about exactly as he pleased, without hindrance of any kind. Again, there is no proof here.

What then remains of the allegations? The imputation that Mme Debacker exploited his religious feelings. But here not one significant fact has been brought forth; Mme Debacker is not shown to have excited a single suspicion on this point. None of the religious allegations listed relates to her; like undue influence with regard to the Convent, they have all been dropped. There is nothing in the charges against her from this point of view.

The charges made against Mme Debacker of having dismissed servants in order to replace them with others more sympathetic to her interests, and of having thus kept Antonio under her control, stand up no better under examination. Not one document in the suit makes possible the admissibility of a single proof. For a period of eighteen months at Tailleville, who was concerned with the hiring and firing of servants? Was it not Antonio? He made inquiries among his friends; he made inquiries of Mme Agnel, begging her for one particularly trustworthy servant who had been with her

110

for years. That particular project must be admitted to have been a very peculiar method for Mme Debacker to have chosen for the purpose of estranging Antonio from his family for purposes of undue influence. In the several letters that were exchanged between Antonio and his cousin, he discussed every detail with perfect mental clarity and a completely independent will. It was only later that he approached the Convent, after the drawing up of the last testament. This matter of searching for servants concerns Antonio alone.

Might he at least have been influenced by Mme Debacker's dismissal of the previous servants? There is no shred of relevant evidence. On the contrary, it is Antonio who is twice seen in the process of dismissing old Amélie and settling her accounts himself, both in January and in February.

On these points, then, there is no evidence other than a vague series of allegations, repudiated by the documentation.

Now we come to a most important aspect of this whole problem of undue influence: the joint residence, the cohabitation of the beneficiary in the house of the testator. But how significant are the objections that can be made to such an arrangement? Concubinage, by itself, does not require the nullification of gifts; for that, it is necessary to prove fraudulent maneuvers as well, as many precedents attest. However regrettable might seem the acts of generosity rewarding the reprehensible career of a concubine [des liberalités couronnant la situation blamable des concubins], magistrates, who are guardians of the law, should resist entanglement with matters of morality, ensuring only that the will of the testator be respected, when freely exercised.

However, even with respect to this serious charge of concubinage, nothing but vague and general allegations are made against Mme Debacker. Though the few counts against her are clearly put forth, for them too the evidence is seriously contradictory, and finally they have only a very slight relevance to the case.

If we look a little further back into Mellerio's life, with the help of this invaluable record that he used for his last ten months, we find him managing through incredible willpower practically to create new limbs for himself. He played music, he drew, he rode, he enjoyed perfect health, he was happy in his love for Mme Debacker. Did she dominate the household? There is not a sign of such control in the entire file of some 200 letters! It was Antonio who administered the estate, tended to business affairs, and dealt on equal terms with specialists of all kinds; he was conspicuously active and clear-headed.

If we look even further, into the domestic economy of the household, we find certain recurrent details that are relevant to the charge that Mme Debacker left him without clothing and even without socks. The file contains his correspondence with tradesmen, and he himself is seen buying household articles, statues, suits—and even socks, if it comes to that.

Through his own initiative he devoted himself to works of charity. There is no impediment to be seen in his amicable relations with friends and relatives.

The constant accumulation of arms by Mme Debacker turns out to consist of one gun that Antonio himself had bought for her because she enjoyed hunting.

Antonio also bought her clothes and gave her a piano. Mellerio's personality is seen to be actively and independently in control of every transaction. Such a display of willpower fills one with admiration.

Reviewing the various acts called into question, the Public Prosecutor states that they all display Antonio's fixed will and his freely expressed intention. They are performed with the cognizance of two honorable notaries, Maîtres Hébert père et fils, and with that of Maître Prevost, who not only discussed them with Antonio but even attempted to dissuade him from performing them. The irregular drawing up of the next-to-last testament is merely the result of the testator's unfamiliarity with legal terminology, and he subsequently redrafted it according to a model provided by a man of integrity. The essential aspect of a man's act is his intention, and with regard to that the notary's intervention can have had no sinister relevance.

The letter from the priest at Garges is merely general advice, applying to no individual in particular.

The conduct of Mellerio, Mme Debacker, the family, and their friends is proof of neither the alleged unsoundness of mind nor the alleged undue influence. Consequently, the evidence is not conclusive. The Public Prosecutor is thus of the opinion that the request for a commission of inquiry should be denied.

So runs a summary of the address in which the issues of this case were examined and evaluated, in what was clearly a remarkable manner.

The delivery of judgment was postponed until next Monday.

[*L'Ordre et la Liberté*, Wednesday, 10 July 1872]

Session of 8 July 1872

The Court has just handed down its judgment, in today's session.

In accordance with the prayers for relief of Mme Debacker and the Convent des Orphelines, and the conclusions of the Public Prosecutor.

The Court has judged, in brief:

That the disputed gifts were the acts of a man in full possession of his intelligence, a firm and fixed will, and perfect liberty.

That, of the evidence submitted in this case, that which was offered in support of this position demonstrated it beyond a reasonable doubt, and that which was offered against it owed its weight to a misleading exaggeration that could not withstand close examination.

That the evidence submitted, being insufficient to establish the required unsoundness of mind, undue influence, and fraudulent maneuvers, is consequently neither relevant nor conclusive.

Therefore, the Court has denied the remedies sought by the Mellerio heirs, both those concerning the requested commission of inquiry and those concerning the nullification of the gifts made to Mme Debacker and the Convent des Orphelines,—has pronounced on various provisory measures,—and has ordered the Mellerio heirs to pay costs.

We hope, one of these days, to be able to offer the text of this legal document at more length [see next chapter], since the few lines given here do not, of course, pretend to be anything more than an inadequate paraphrase.

4

The 1872 Judgment

[This document is the full text of the court's judgment, taken from *Jurisprudence Normande: Receuil des Arrêts des Cours d'Appel de Caen et de Rouen* (Vol. 38, 1874). This publication, as the subtitle states, is an annual collection of the decisions of these two courts of appeal, so its primary concern was to present the 1873 appeal decision (see chapter 6). But the case was so "important" that the editors felt that their readers would be interested in having a fuller acquaintance with the issues of the original trial than could be given in the usual short summary, so they included a verbatim transcript of the original judgment. They provided the following headnote:]

TESTAMENT.—Unsoundness of Mind.—Proof.—Listing of Allegations.—Private Papers.—Correspondence.—Undue Influence.—Deceitful and Fraudulent Maneuvers.—Concubinage.

When a testament is contested on grounds of the unsoundness of mind of the testator and fraudulent maneuvers against him, when allegations are listed, specified, and submitted in evidence in support of such grounds, the Court may nevertheless reject such evidence if it appears to them, according to documents submitted in the case, particularly according to the correspondence and private papers of the testator (such as notebooks, agendas, and account books) that he enjoyed full play of his intellectual powers and that he did in fact have the capacity to make a testament (*Civil Code*, Article 901).

The exercise of undue influence cannot be invoked as grounds of nullification of a testament unless there is evidence of fraud, that is, of manipulative practices or deceptions that have weakened and altered the intention of the testator.

Concubinage cannot be invoked as grounds of undue influence in order to nullify a testament.

(Mellerio Heirs v. *la dame* Debacker and the Convent of Notre-Dame-de-la-Délivrande.)

(Caen, Civil Court, 9 July 1872)

We have thought it necessary to reproduce in full the judgment of the Court of Caen; our readers will thus be provided with an exact account of both the facts of this important case and the legal issues that this appeal decision has implicitly ruled on, in relation to the grounds of judgment invoked by the judges of the original case.

[The text of the judgment itself, as is customary in French judicial procedure, contains a full discussion of the relative merits of the issues and arguments of the case. As David and de Vries remark, "With the exception of the *cours d'assises*, French courts are compelled by law to set forth the reasons underlying their decisions, which are read aloud in public audience" (*The French Legal System*, p. 36). In the text of this judgment, the following sections are of particular interest:

—the court's awareness of the extent of the heirs' reliance on the Pasquier affidavit (pp. 117–18 below);

—the refusal even to consider whether Mellerio's death was voluntary or accidental (p. 118);

—the remark that since Mellerio's earlier testaments were uncontested, the only real question at issue can be how large Mme Debacker's portion of the estate should be (p. 119);

—the complete text of the famous letter of 10 August 1869 to Maître Prevost, in which Mellerio defended his decision to leave his estate to Mme Debacker and the poor (p. 121);

—the close scrutiny of individual allegations (pp. 123–27);

—the swipe at the heirs for having deliberately given vague and misleading dates to their allegations (p. 127).

On the whole, the verdict seems a remarkably fair, subtle, and lucid piece of reasoning. Except for the usual archaic *la dame, le sieur*, and so forth, and words and phrases in brackets, all italics are the court's.]

Judgment

Considering that the Mellerio heirs seek, in their principal demands, that the Court declare henceforth null and void:

1) Every gift made to *la dame* Debacker by Antonio Mellerio, regardless of the date on which such acts occurred but particularly that of 21 October 1869;

Further, that they be authorized to prove the facts listed by them;

Considering that the Mellerio heirs base their demand for nullification:

1) *On the unsoundness of mind of the testator;*

2) *On the fraudulent maneuvers* practiced by *la dame* Debacker, the Missionary Fathers, and the Convent of Notre Dame de la Charité de la Délivrande, to influence the testator to make bequests in their favor;

Considering that, in order to prove Antonio Mellerio's unsoundness of mind, the plaintiffs rely primarily on the affidavit of Dr. Pasquier, dated 23 August 1870;

That the doctor certifies:

1) That in October 1867 he had treated Antonio Mellerio; that he had diagnosed obvious mental disorder, as manifested in an extremely pronounced erotic delirium;

2) That in January 1868, the day after the burial of his mother, Antonio, moved by an impulse of expiation, deliberately and severely burned his hands; Dr. Pasquier, having been summoned immediately, found extensive lesions; the hands were completely carbonized; and Antonio recovered after several months;

3) That after his recovery, Antonio returned to his residence at Tailleville, after having been approached by the person whom he had repudiated; and on 13 April 1870 he threw himself from the belvedere of his château and shattered his skull;

That, from all the facts cited above, Dr. Pasquier concludes: that there is very clear evidence that Antonio Mellerio suffered from obvious mental disorder, which resulted in suicide; that consequently he attests, in sworn statement, that Antonio Mellerio had no cognizance of his actions, and that he was unable to understand whatever arrangements or bequests he may have made later than 1867. In testimony to which this affidavit was drawn up;

Considering that the above affidavit, which was obviously

117

delivered to the Mellerio heirs in order to facilitate the annulment of acts and bequests of Antonio Mellerio made *later than* 1867, only establishes two certain facts, to wit:

Antonio's sudden seizure of October 1867;

And the dramatic scene of 11 January 1868;

That it was rash and erroneous of Dr. Pasquier to *assume* that the event of 13 April 1870 was suicide, and to conclude that Antonio had no cognizance of his actions;

That no one can be certain whether the death of Antonio Mellerio was *voluntary* or *accidental*;

Considering that whatever may be the contrast between the disdainful remarks made by Dr. Pasquier concerning *la dame* Debacker in the above-mentioned affidavit and those of letters he wrote to Antonio on 19 and 27 June, 3 August, and 1 October 1868, containing the following passages: *"My very best regards to our friend Anna." "Please embrace our mutual friend for me." "I clasp you and Anna to my heart." "Please give my fondest regards to your devoted companion"*—nevertheless, this document does contain one fact of undeniable importance with respect to the question of soundness of mind: that on 11 January 1868, in a fit of delirium, Antonio Mellerio did deliberately burn off both his hands;

Considering that the question before the Court, reduced to its simplest terms, is to decide whether or not Antonio Mellerio did, after the terrible scene of 11 January 1868, recover the necessary soundness of mind to be able to make a deed of gift either *inter vivos* or by testament;

That it is therefore necessary to examine and evaluate the major documents submitted in the case;

Considering that, from 1853 to 1870, Antonio Mellerio and *la dame* Debacker lived together under the same roof;

That these illicit relations, though condemned by morality, *do not ever*, UNDER THE LAW, *constitute grounds for nullification*; in a word, concubinage does not ever constitute *grounds of incapacity* chargeable against a testator, always excepting acts of undue influence or fraud that might serve to taint an act of generosity made in the concubine's favor;

Considering that, by handwritten testament of 27 February 1865, Antonio Mellerio, who had received 300,000 francs from his father's estate, bequeathed *one hundred twenty thousand francs* to *la dame* Debacker; that the Mellerio heirs have not produced a single document or a single piece of evidence from which it could be inferred that *at that time* the testator did not enjoy the full play of his mental faculties, or that *la dame* Debacker had practiced fraudulent maneuvers to obtain the legacy;

That, consequently, the Mellerio heirs and *la dame* Debacker are at present contesting *only the amount* of the gifts of the testator;

Considering that, on 6 January 1868, the day after his mother's death, Antonio Mellerio bequeathed to *la dame* Debacker *one hundred fifty thousand francs*;

That, by a testament dated 4 June 1868, he gave her half his estate;

That this testament carries the following *post-script*: "This testament was written in my presence at Tailleville this very day by M. Mellerio, with his mouth, and was given by him to me immediately. Signed: Hébert";

That this note, written by Maître Hébert, then notary at Douvres, is of considerable importance in the case; that, indeed, it comes from a public officer to whose integrity everyone has paid tribute; that it does not merely attest to a material fact, to wit: that Mellerio had written the testament with his lips; but that it implies especially that Maître Hébert had wished, over and above his usual professional habits, to attest clearly that this testament was the work of a man enjoying all his mental faculties; that this act was the expression of a free and considered intention; that to interpret otherwise the note transcribed above would be to assume an act of senile compliance to which Maître Hébert, whose integrity and independence of character were known to all, would never have lent himself;

Considering that, by an act of 17 September 1868, Antonio Mellerio bestowed on *la dame* Debacker an annuity of 12,000 francs;

That, on 18 June 1869, he bequeathed her his entire estate, with the property at Tailleville in life estate only;

That finally, on 21 October 1869, he bequeathed her his entire estate, with the property of Tailleville and 200,000

119

francs to be left, after her death, to the Convent of Notre Dame de la Délivrande;

Considering that these successive and similar acts, containing gifts whose value rises as the fortune of the testator increases, demonstrate, beyond a reasonable doubt, that their author had a fixed intention to favor her to whom he referred in his letters as "his good angel," and whom he wished to recompense for the care and affection that she had consistently shown for him;

Considering that it is an established fact that, thanks to superhuman energy and perseverance, Antonio eventually succeeded in writing and drawing with the help of artificial hands: "*It is a veritable resurrection*," wrote Maître Prevost, family lawyer and friend; that the letters of Morel, an employee of the Mellerio family, observe that from 30 January 1868 on: "his mental condition continues to improve"; "That the poor invalid's mental condition is fine"; "That he is improving in every respect"; "That he is not at all insane"; "That the doctors are opposed to having him declared incompetent";

That it is equally clear that the family did not take any of the precautions that they should have taken if the delirium of 11 January 1868 had really continued; that Antonio's mother had in her testament entailed the disposable portion of her estate, bequeathing half of this portion to any children of Antonio's, born or unborn, that all the property was sold, and thus that property which joint-ownership would have protected against alienation became available to the *de cuius* for disposal;

Considering that Antonio Mellerio continued to administer his estate, as the numerous acts that figure in the case attest: sales, purchases, loans, grantings of proxies;

That finally, Antoine and Joseph Mellerio themselves recognized Antonio's competency; that the stock and goodwill belonging to Antonio's business were bought by Joseph, and the assessment of their value was done by Antoine; obviously, the plaintiffs would not have had business dealings with Antonio if he had been in fact a victim of madness;

Considering, finally, that the following letters (from which we must cite extracts) throw a brilliant light both on the soundness of Antonio Mellerio's mind and on his fixed intention to make his testament in favor of *la dame* Debacker and the orphan girls of la Délivrande:

"My dear friend," wrote Maître Prevost, to whom Antonio had sent his proposed testament, "I am sorry not to fulfill your request, on the plain grounds that I am completely opposed to it; I must tell you, in all candor, that you are making a serious mistake: one should not deprive one's family for the sake of a mistress and a religious establishment. That is my feeling on the subject";

Considering that, whatever the above advice may be—and on its merits it is not appropriate for the Court to comment—it was certainly offered by a devoted friend; that in any case it was bound to make a great impression on the intention and will of a man who all agree was extremely weakened in both body and mind; that, nevertheless, it did not;

That, on 10 August 1869, Antonio responded, "My dear friend, you use the word 'deprive' [*dépouiller*], which I could understand, if it applied to one's children, but not as applied to cousins who are richer than I, and especially not for remote relations who have never had any feeling for me and who would only laugh if they were my legatees. If I were married and had children, would my cousins be my legatees? No, of course not. And so, since I will not marry, I adopt the poor as my children. As for my good angel whom I have with me, the word you have used [*maîtresse*] is hateful. Anna has exercised no influence on me—no one has advised me. The entire idea is mine alone—I am only doing my duty as an honorable man by naming Anna to be my legatee and to continue my work. Who is with me? Who cares for me? Who gives me her life? My dear Anna. Neither you, nor I, nor anyone sees into her heart. But for more than the year that I have been here, has anyone in my family troubled themselves to discover if I were happy? No, not one. I tell you all this, my dear friend, so that you may be convinced that nothing will change my mind. So return the testament to me immediately so that I may have it formally drawn up."

Considering, that if the contents of this letter, in which the grounds for the bequests contained in the testament of 21 October 1869 are heavily emphasized, are compared with the

121

holograph of 18 June of the same year, which is really nothing more than a rough draft of the testament of 21 October, the main focus of the case, it is clear that the last testament of 1869 was a long-premeditated action [this question of handwriting would be a major issue in the 1873 appeal];

That, if one examines the numerous letters written by Antonio between January 1868 and October 1869, one may find there the spirit of his earlier years, but now more sober—the lively imagination of the better days of his past, without the erotic stories and images that tarnished the correspondence of his youth; that there is not a word, a phrase, or a thought to be seen that betrays the least incoherence or mental disturbance; that all the documents reveal that Antonio Mellerio was in complete possession of his rational faculties;

Considering that the above opinion is confirmed by correspondence from the testator's friends and relations; that they all congratulate him on the speed of his recovery and on the complete happiness he enjoys with his devoted companion; that these same relations thank him effusively for services he has done for them, services that they go so far as to call favors; that those who thus perceived in him the competency to do business to their benefit cannot now logically turn and contest his competency to make a testament;

Considering that the plaintiffs rely vainly on certain expressions employed in the proposition made by them to *la dame* Debacker [the attempt to reach a compromise settlement out of court after Mellerio's death (p. 49)]; that this transaction, which aimed at the avoidance of the present lawsuit by mutual concession, shows that *la dame* Debacker admits that Antonio did perform some eccentric acts; that her acknowledgment of the scene of 11 January 1868 does not significantly alter the case; that finally, if the Court were to approve of this arrangement suggested by the Mellerio heirs, including their large concession to her of a life annuity of 10,000 francs, while if at the same time it were to let stand the sizable bequest to the Convent of la Délivrande, the heirs would not derive any very clear advantage;

That, moreover, to find in a preliminary draft of an invalid document an admission that would amount to a formal renunciation of the rights of one of the contracting parties would be completely to distort the intention of the transaction;

That the conclusion to be drawn from the above material, insofar as it relates to the principal question, is that the documents submitted as evidence, far from establishing the unsoundness of mind of Antonio Mellerio, *prove on the contrary, that on the date of 21 October 1869 he was competent to make a testament.*

On the second charge, that concerning undue influence:

Considering that the plaintiffs have not produced a single document from which it might be inferred that *la dame* Debacker had practiced fraudulent maneuvers to obtain the bequests made in her favor;

Considering that only insignificant letters, which could not have any bearing on the case, have been cited against the *Missionary Fathers, who are not parties in the case,* and the nuns of the Convent of la Délivrande; that the letters between Antonio and one nun of the Convent, involving an unsuccessful search for a cook, could not possibly constitute acts of fraudulent pressure on a testator to obtain bequests;

Considering, finally, that in their arguments the Mellerio heirs have admitted that the documents produced by them on their behalf are not at all sufficient for a nullification *de plano* of the testaments at issue, arguing rather that they establish presumptions that make necessary, according to them, the commission of inquiry that they seek;

As far as this charge is concerned:

Considering that the allegations cited by the heirs are no more than a *detailed and exaggerated reproduction of the documents submitted in argument;*

That actually, the allegations listed in numbers *one through seven*, relating to the dissolute passions and extravagant expenses of Antonio Mellerio and to the origins of his relations with *la dame* Debacker, are all taken from letters that Antonio wrote to his brother Victor, then residing at Turin;

That it is an established fact that, if Antonio Mellerio did indulge in deplorable excesses with all the fire and impetuosity of his youth and personality; that if, through his wealth and physical advantages his amorous conquests were

123

too many and too easy, there is nothing in the correspondence in which he confides his deplorable successes to indicate that his intelligence was affected thereby;

That the habits of dissipation and gambling with which he is reproached amount to modest winnings if he was lucky and modest losses if he was not; that a close examination of the letters reveals that if he was often tipsy with Roger the opera singer, he was never completely drunk;

That all these allegations, as well as the romantic [*romanesque*] detail of his encounter and subsequent liaison with *la dame* Debacker, are irrelevant to the outcome of the case;

Considering that the extravagant expenses charged to *la dame* Debacker at the beginning of her liaison with Mellerio are denied by the documents of the case;

That, while admitting that *la dame* Debacker used her influence to convince Antonio Mellerio to leave Paris and take up residence at Tailleville, this fact is evidence neither of a mental aberration on the part of Antonio Mellerio nor of a fraudulent maneuver on the part of *la dame* Debacker; that these projects are explained by the awkward position in Paris in which they were placed by their intimate relationship;

Considering that the allegations listed under numbers *nine to twenty-six* are concerned to establish the fever of October 1867 and the delirium of 1868; that these facts have been admitted as established in the case and have been so considered by the Court; that consequently further proof of these facts is superfluous;

Considering that the remark attributed to *la dame* Debacker in number *twenty-nine* of the list, in that she is alleged to have said to some friends, "Oh, if I had listened to you, I would now be wretchedly poor with your miserable annuity, but now I have him!" *is completely implausible*;

That it was revealed in argument that these alleged reproaches were supposedly addressed to *Morel*, the financial agent of the Mellerios; that no one could explain why this person, who should have been outraged by her disgraceful remark, then asked in his letters to Antonio that his appreciation be forwarded to Anna for her devoted care, and sent her his best regards;

That while recognizing that MOREL has sworn to such

facts, his letters give good cause for suspecting the honesty of such testimony.

That, moreover, all the documents in the case prove that the project of undue influence, which the above alleged remark seems to announce, was never realized; that the letters written by members of the Mellerio family, by friends of Antonio, by Maître Prevost, and even by Dr. Pasquier, contain nothing but praise for the affection and concern that *la dame* Debacker never ceased to display for their friend Antonio;

Considering that, in numbers *thirty, thirty-one, thirty-two, thirty-three, thirty-four* and *forty-one* of their list, the Mellerio heirs seek to prove specifically: that almost daily communication was established between the château of Tailleville, the Missionary Fathers of la Délivrande and the Convent of la Vierge-Fidèle; that, with the assistance of *la dame* Debacker, they soon managed completely to dominate the will of Antonio Mellerio so as to make whatever changes in his domestic staff might facilitate their project; that to this end the Convent of la Délivrande was charged with, and accepted, the responsibility of finding servants for the château of Tailleville, and of making information available about the inhabitants of the château for the purpose of hiring servants to work therein; that *la dame* Debacker had the most whole-hearted cooperation from a Father *Joseph*, who constantly agitated Antonio's imagination by threatening him with hell and the Devil;

That all this wealth [*ce luxe*] of detail is *based on two short letters* between Antonio Mellerio and a nun of the Convent, concerning a search for two servants that his cousin *la dame* Agnel had been unable to obtain for him;

That Father JOSEPH *is a mysterious person* whom the Mellerio heirs have not been able to identify for their opponents, who have repeatedly asked the plaintiffs for specific details on this subject in order to defend themselves;

Considering, furthermore, that the attorney for the Mellerio heirs has *openly and publicly declared* in his argument that he had never intended to charge the Convent with undue influence; that, on their parts, *there existed none of the shame of exercising undue influence*;

That it necessarily and logically follows from this admission that the above allegations can no longer concern *la dame* Debacker either, since the role of undue influence in the above allegations involves her collusion with the Missionary Fathers and the Sisters of la Délivrande;

Considering that the allegations listed as numbers *thirty-five* and *thirty-six* are taken from the correspondence between Antonio Mellerio and the priest of Garges, a friend of his mother's, with whom he consulted about obtaining a chaplain to say mass at the chapel of Tailleville, and of whom he made inquiries about the entail to which part of his estate was subject;

That a glance at the letters of Antonio Mellerio is sufficient to show that there is not a single sign of mental aberration therein;

Considering that the *thirty-seventh* allegation, which is undated, concerns Antonio's purchasing exclusively religious books, and drawing exclusively religious pictures [in the allegation it is actually only implied, not stated, that the drawings were exclusively religious];

That these allegations are not only insignificant but the result of obvious exaggeration; that, as a matter of fact, there have been drawings by Antonio Mellerio submitted in evidence that have no religious character at all [a reference to the sketch of cupids sent by Antonio to Mme Debacker while he was recovering from burning off his hands];

Considering that numbers *thirty-eight, thirty-nine, forty, forty-two, forty-four, forty-five, forty-six, forty-seven, fifty,* and *fifty-one* concern allegations contained in an affidavit of a man named Jousse, a traveling musician who had received cordial hospitality from Antonio Mellerio and *la dame* Debacker, a hospitality he was quite soon obliged to forgo, on account of a letter written to Antonio Mellerio by one of the creditors of this indigent man; that Jousse bitterly complained about this dismissal; that it is strange that this man should have thus spontaneously offered his testimony; that it is no less strange that the Mellerio heirs should produce this affidavit, thus renouncing the legal advantages of regularly introduced testimony [the exact implication of this remark remains obscure; presumably, by the use of a formal affidavit from Jousse on this occasion, the family was barred from

126

using his oral testimony in a commision of inquiry, should one be ordered; it is possible that the heirs resorted to this tactic of introducing an affidavit either because Jousse made a sorry impression in person or because he was liable to prove embarrassing under cross-examination];

That in number *fifty* may be seen reappearing the ghost of *Father Joseph*, whom it is impossible to identify and concerning whom the Mellerio heirs have refused to give any information;

Considering, finally, that the Mellerio heirs seek to prove (numbers *forty-nine*, *fifty-two*, and *fifty-three*), that *la dame* Debacker forced the servants of the château to leave, either because they were terrified of her or because they defended their master;

That these allegations are shown to be false by the documents submitted, which demonstrate that it was almost exclusively Antonio Mellerio who was concerned with the domestic administration of the château and the supervision of its personnel; that he had in every matter complete liberty and absolute independence;

Considering that, in order to avoid giving precise dates to the allegations listed under numbers *forty* to *fifty-three*, dates the inclusion of which, in the eventuality of a commission of inquiry, would permit their opponents to defend themselves, the Mellerio heirs took care to add: that these events occurred during the months of August, September, and October 1868; that they also add, in number *fifty-four*, that during October 1868 he bathed in a large tub of water, which he called a bath of purification;

That, to do justice to these later additions to the original allegations it is sufficient to remark that they are not specifically dated; that they may thus be assumed to have occurred later than the last testament;

Considering, moreover, that even if it be acknowledged that more or less honest and intelligent witnesses have testified in support of the allegations made by the Mellerio heirs, their testimony is invalidated by the letter of 10 August [1869] cited above;

That this document proves conclusively that the testator made his testament of 21 October 1869 in favor neither of the

Missionary Fathers nor of the Convent of Notre Dame de la
Charité; that it was *to the poor*, whom he adopted as his
children, that he gave the splendid property of Tailleville;
that in making *la dame* Debacker his legatee he was rewarding not a mistress but a devoted companion who had remained by his side, who had cared for him and who had kept
him alive; that the man who wrote this letter and made the
testament of 21 October 1869 was sound of mind and free
from any external influence;

Considering, moreover, that the Court should order a
commission of inquiry only with extreme circumspection;
that although undoubtedly, in the case in point, a commission of inquiry is a legitimate means of investigation, it
should nevertheless not be forgotten that in cases of common
law the legislature in Article 1341 of the *Civil Code* has
hedged admission of evidence [in commissions of inquiry]
with rigorous conditions that suggest its justifiable distrust
of such a dubious measure;

That it follows from all the above, that, disregarding the
subsidiary plea [the request to be allowed to bring witnesses
in a commission of inquiry, in order to prove the listed alle-
gations] the Court should deny the claims of the Mellerio
heirs brought against *la dame* Debacker and the Convent of
Notre Dame de la Charité des Orphelines de Marie de la
Délivrande.

On these grounds,

the COURT, disregarding the request for a commission of
inquiry, denies the claim brought by *les sieurs* Jean Mellerio
and others against *la dame* Debacker and against the Convent of Notre Dame de la Charité des Orphelines de Marie de
la Délivrande; and grants *la dame* Debacker possession of the
legacy in her favor contained in the testament of 21 October
1869.

9 July 1872. Civil Court of Caen—First Chamber—
President, Maître Pellerin—Judgment confirmed, Maître
Cosnards-Desclozets, Public Prosecutor.

Appeal by the Mellerio heirs.

5

Strategies of Discrepancy

The preceding chapter concludes that portion of the study which presents documents containing raw material for *Red Cotton Night-Cap Country*. At this point it may be useful to stand back a moment to examine some of the clarifications of theme and structure that may be gained by comparing the poem with material from which it was derived. As must already be apparent, in Browning's version of this history there are many omissions and distortions of this material, large and small. Some of these merely help simplify a complex narrative, but others contribute to the creation of effects that often differ in important ways from those made by the original documents in the case. Thus, as in any source study, these documents can be very useful in suggesting what themes the writer had determined that his material would convey, especially since, in this particular poem, so much depends on Browning's insistence on the strictness of his fidelity to publicly verifiable facts. Given that reiterated insistence, he presumably made any departures from those public facts only with a certain reluctance.

There already has been cited, in the Introduction, a passage from one of Browning's letters explaining that "the facts are so exactly put down" in *Red Cotton Night-Cap Country* that he was required to change the names of persons and places "in order to avoid the possibility of prosecution for Libel—that is, telling the exact truth" (p. 16). Indeed, he later went so far as to draw up an "Advertisement," "prepared, one may assume, as a foreword,"[1] in which he defended all the material in the poem as "depending absolutely on public authority." This document, Browning's most unequivocal statement of his strict adherence to the historical facts as he found them given, "as they were presented to and decided upon by the Court of the Country, as they exist in print and as they may be procured by anybody," is given in full on page three of this volume.

In the poem itself this note of factual demonstration is struck from the very beginning, as Browning and his lady friend tour the Tailleville district of the Normandy coast, long before he even starts to tell the story of the Mellerios. He points out in the distance the tower of la Délivrande, which "you front now, lady!" (1.436). The crown recently placed on the statue of the Virgin, "you must see!" (1.512). When they come to "reconnoitring" (1.563) the Mellerio château, "Let us complete our survey, go right round / The place" (1.695–96). When the tale itself is finally reached, Browning's recital is heavily laced with such comments as: "I find [this account of Antonio's youthful escapades] deposed / At [Caen], confirmed in his own words" (2.316–17). So "runs on the confidence, / Poor fellow, that was read in open Court" (2.395–96). And when he reports the statements Mellerio made after burning off his hands, "I quote / The words, I cannot give the smile" (3.457–58). There are many more such instances of claims to literal accuracy, but these examples will serve to illustrate Browning's repeated concern to be perceived as consistently retailing demonstrable historical fact. A further guarantee of his objectivity is his confession in book two that his researches have occasionally been confusing: Mellerio's letters discuss Mme Debacker's early history "in a style / To puzzle Court Guide students, much more me" (2.547–48). This remark confirms both Browning's amateur status as an investigator and his claim to have no access to any privileged information. Perhaps his most useful tactic in this regard is his ostentatious honesty in clearly labeling certain occasional passages of subjective interpretation: "What follows you are free to disbelieve: / It may be true or false . . . (3.217–18); "I give it you as mere conjecture, mind!" (3.255). The effect of such scrupulous asides is to suggest that wherever they do not occur the narrative is strictly objective, and that there the reader is *not* free to disbelieve what follows. This implication is not true, to a remarkable degree, and a survey of the more significant departures from his original shows that Browning was often prepared to distort his raw material as much as necessary, in order to force it to yield the themes he wished it to, in spite of his recurrent claims to complete factuality. The most important discrepancies, which this chapter will examine, naturally occur in the presentation of the three main figures: Mellerio and the two personifications of his emotional dilemma— Mme Debacker and the Convent of la Délivrande.

ANTONIO MELLERIO (LÉONCE MIRANDA)

With regard to Mellerio, Browning's major alterations of original material relate to his determination for this character to embody one of his favorite themes. Mellerio, like Norbert or Clive, is to be an example of moral evolution at work, displaying the progressive clarification of a moral issue until the point is reached where further ponderings, shifts, and compromises are no longer possible, and decisive action must be taken. In this instance the struggle occurs between Mellerio's romantic affections and his religious convictions, symbolized throughout the poem by the flowery turf and stark towers of the poem's subtitle. In Browning's view Mellerio had realized from his earliest years that it was the goal of his life eventually to prefer the ultimate truths of religion to the transient pleasures of this world, but he was so torn between these alternatives that his entire life, up to its last day, was a series of various efforts to reconcile the two so as to avoid having to choose between them. To Browning this evasiveness is a basic human folly: "Life's business [is] just the terrible choice," as the Pope remarks in *The Ring and the Book* (10.1237). So he applauds Antonio's final leap as being at last a courageous, if misguided, commitment to a moral choice.

Consequently, Browning's theme was well served by having Mellerio's entire life perceived as a coherent sequence of lessons leading up to that culminating leap,[2] but the truth is that to impose this pattern on the events of Mellerio's life, as recorded in the original documents, required Browning to distort the testimony his source material offered him. The events themselves, "reported in the newspaper" (4.31) as

Browning boasts he found them, simply do not warrant much confidence in the interpretation he wished to give them. For instance, it was useful for Browning to have Mellerio's cold bath in the Seine, in October 1867, play a role much more important than even the heirs had hoped to establish. They only sought to trace in that episode "the first symptoms of that unsoundness of mind of which the last stage would be suicide" (p. 41); but Browning saw it as showing Mellerio remorsefully ending the thoughtless, irresponsible phase of his life by seeking an easy escape from his mother's reproaches. In Browning's hands the bath became nothing less than attempted suicide itself, a "remedy / For fever, in a cold Autumnal flow" (3.109);

> "Go and be rid of memory in a bath!"
> Craftily whispered [the Devil,] Who besets the ear
> On such occasions.

> (3.110–12)

Browning's version is demonstrably inconsistent with the literal sense of the documentation at several points. As regards Mellerio's bath being a response to his mother's reproaches for having restored Tailleville so expensively, Browning there illegitimately elevated to fact an unsupported allegation of the heirs, even though, as the defense pointed out, "Letters submitted to the Court [by the defendants] show that Mme Mellerio approved both the plans and the expense; on one occasion she even reproached Antonio for the apparent diffidence with which he asked her for money!" (pp. 54, 102). And as regards the claim that the bath was itself a suicide attempt, that is so implausible that the heirs could not bring themselves even to allege it, though if they could have, it would have been ideally suited to their case. Further, although Browning does mention that in the course of Mellerio's recovery he lay "Raving" (3.115), he did not include the most dramatic moment of that episode, when Mellerio "enter[ed] his jewelry shop wrapped in a sheet like a cloak, with his head circled by a handkerchief like a crown, raving of his coming glories" (p. 84). The ludicrous egotism implied by these details is very much at odds with Browning's interpretation of the event as Mellerio's first despondent

solution to his increasingly painful inability to choose between the contradictory values symbolized by his mother and
his mistress. To have included them would have made that
interpretation seem painfully farfetched.

After this crisis, according to Browning, Mellerio's life divided itself into two stages of increasingly enlightened moral
growth. His first attempt at resolving his dilemma was to
ignore the claims of religion entirely, "To build up, independent of the towers, / A durable pavilion o'er the turf"
(3.680–81). When this plan "issued in [the] disaster" (3.682)
of the destruction of his hands, Browning sees Mellerio as
having learned a valuable lesson, "By process I respect if not
admire" (3.657), and as turning with renewed determination
and increased insight to his second "experiment" (3.1057),
an effort to harmonize the two claims, "by tunnel, or else
gallery, / . . . And never try complete abandonment / Of
one or other" (3.684–88). This last phase of Mellerio's education would end in the leap from the belvedere, and for that
leap to be positively climactic, Browning needed Mellerio's
last two years to be seen as increasingly vigorous and
healthy, so that Mellerio could begin his soliloquy on the
belvedere with the joyous observation that he was then "In
prime of life, perfection of estate / Bodily [and] mental"
(4.36–37). The problem for an objective reporter was that
though Mellerio had undoubtedly made a complete recovery—"It is truly a resurrection!" (p. 72), marveled the
attorney for the convent—he equally undoubtedly also experienced many episodes of physical feebleness and mental
"eccentricity" (p. 49). These it suited Browning's purpose
to gloss over, thus giving in his version the impression that
Mellerio's physical and mental health was much more consistently vigorous than the documents themselves suggest.

For instance, soon after his recovery Mellerio sold to his
cousins by auction his share of the jewelry business. In the
trial it was frequently stressed, and fully acknowledged, that
Mellerio good-naturedly gave his cousins every possible advantage in these negotiations. Not only did he publicly stip-
ulate a minimum price of 200,000 francs so as to keep other
bidders away, but he also permitted the cousins to be the only
assessors of the property they were buying, and he further

133

granted a delay of payment of the principal for 10 years (for details see pp. 57, 73–74, 106). Though a good case might easily be made for shady dealing on the part of the cousins, Mellerio himself was extremely generous. But to avoid, I take it, any hint of lingering sentimental weakness in his hero, Browning created for Mellerio's role in the sale a fierce aggressiveness fully the equal of his cousins'. In the poem, without the slightest justification, Browning had Mellerio insist that "the price [be] adjudged / By experts I shall have assistance from" (3.598–99), and concluded the episode by remarking that the jewelry business was eventually "bought by them and sold by him on terms . . . might serve 'twixt wolf and wolf,' / Substitute 'bit and clawed' for 'signed and sealed' " (3.624–26). Where the original event could legitimately have been taken as implying for Mellerio a role of passive compliance, Browning showed only an immediate and entire resumption of alertness and energy.

In the poem this depiction of undimmed intelligence and energy continues unabated to the end of Mellerio's life, in spite of the court's observation in its judgment that Mellerio in his last two years was "a man who all agree was extremely weakened in both body and mind" (p. 121). Of all the various eccentricities attributed to Mellerio in the suit, only one, his journey to la Délivrande on his knees, found its way into the poem, where for all its peculiarity it was merely labeled an instance of Mellerio's "Spiritual effort" (3.1004) and "incessant . . . devotion" (3.1020). "According to his lights, I praise the man" (3.1019), says Browning; and Mellerio's increasingly vivid awareness of the religious dimension of life is the key, in Browning's view, to understanding his climactic leap from the belvedere. Whereas the defense dismissed Mellerio's death as a simple accident and the plaintiffs insisted it was lunatic suicide, Browning discovered a typically perverse interpretation, in which he accepted the hostile premises of the heirs but used them to arrive at a radically different conclusion. Agreeing with the heirs that Mellerio's motive was an absurdly exaggerated religious conviction, Browning nevertheless saw that act not as the final proof of idiocy but as the best and sanest gesture of Mellerio's whole life.

134

> At any rate, I see no slightest sign
> Of folly (let me tell you in advance),
> Nothing but wisdom meets me manifest
> In the procedure of the Twentieth Day
> Of April, 'Seventy,—folly's year in France.
>
> (3.1065–69)

Browning saw the leap as a courageous, even rational, solution to Mellerio's arrival at the tormented conviction that the basic cause of his suffering was the inadequacy of his faith in the Virgin's infinite love. "Therefore, to prove indubitable faith" (4.264) in her forgiveness, he jumped, so that she might perform the miracle of permitting him to fly from the château to the church of la Délivrande. And Browning wholeheartedly approved: Mellerio was not mad but

> sane, I say.
> Such being the conditions of his life,
> Such end of life was not irrational.
> Hold a belief, you only half-believe,
> With all-momentous issues either way,—
> And I advise you imitate this leap,
> Put faith to proof, be cured or killed at once!
>
> (4.340–46)

Now, it is true, of course, that this interpretation is presented not as a general consensus but as Browning's own private inference from the public record; and I think it is one of the major themes of this work, as it was for *The Ring and the Book*, that it is in fact possible for an imaginative sympathy to have valid insights into "pure, crude fact" (*Ring*, 1.85), as the *Old Yellow Book* was there described. But the success of the demonstration of that faculty very much depends, as it did in *The Ring and the Book*, on the reader's sense that the narrator is reliably objective; and in *Red Cotton Night-Cap Country*, as we have begun to see, that reliability is much more a calculated impression than an actual fact. In this climactic leap, for example, Browning did not faithfully reproduce its circumstances, but instead carefully stage-managed the details of the incident so as to increase the plausibility of his own interpretation. For instance, in keeping with his emphasis on Mellerio's vigorous mental and

135

physical health, Browning endowed Mellerio with a mood on his last day so flamboyantly exuberant as to make any suggestion of suicide completely unlikely. The documents agree (pp. 46, 60) that Mellerio had just ordered a carriage for a morning drive, but in Browning's version this drive in a carriage became a ride on the horse, and not on just any horse, but "a wild young horse to exercise, / And teach the way to go and pace to keep" (3.1072–73). The newspaper accounts assume that Mellerio went up to the belvedere after bidding farewell to Mme Debacker while the carriage was being prepared. This simple action became in Browning's hands an elated "clearing, two and two, / The staircase-steps" with "elastic foot" (3.1083–84, 4.6), after closing Mme Debacker's door "considerately" (3.1081), presumably so as not to imply any manic lack of control.

After such an introduction, any reasonable reader can only agree with Browning that suicide must seem out of the question. As for what really happened on the balcony, in the actual trial there appeared a very interesting piece of evidence that Browning chose to omit completely. According to Mme Debacker's attorney,

> The balustrade was 1.03 meters higher than the floor of the belvedere. There has been testimony that on that day a lead roller, 8 centimeters in diameter, had been left on the platform, inside the balustrade, on the side from which Antonio fell. What happened there? Did Antonio wish to stand on this roller, with nothing higher than the balustrade of 95 centimeters (103 minus 8) for support? Did he lean forward too far, to see the carriage or some other object of his attention? And then—tall and strong, but with both hands mutilated—did he lose his balance? This is the most plausible explanation. There were no witnesses. (P. 61).

The presence of the roller certainly raises awkward questions that can never arise in Browning's version, since it does not appear there. And as for whether or not there were witnesses, Browning subtly altered the evidence of Richer, the gardener, who testified to the police at the time that, "while working in the park about 60 meters from the château, he heard a thud and then saw in the garden walk the body of Mellerio, whose skull was cracked; he thought Mellerio probably fell accidentally" (p. 166).[3] So, as Mme Debacker's attorney mentioned above, there were no witnesses to the actual event. But in Browning's poem, "A gardener who watched, at work the while / Dibbling a flower-bed for geranium-shoots, / Saw the catastrophe" (4.342–44). The difference, though slight, is important because if the gardener really had been watching the whole episode, then what he saw, according to Browning, was "A sublime spring *from* the balustrade" (4.338, italics mine). This phrase could only describe a deliberate leap, hardly an awkward accidental tumble *over* the balustrade, so that Browning's version of Richer's testimony has a shifted focus that effectively denies the possibility of accident that the original so strongly implies. The opinion of the gardener and the lawyer—that Mellerio's death was most probably accidental—is confirmed in the impartial summary of the public prosecutor: "The circumstances of the site, the maimed condition of the man, the possibility of vertigo—all combine to make an accident extremely plausible. Though indeed, considering all the possibilities it would be foolhardy to claim certain knowledge one way or another" (p. 102). In Browning's version, although he kept unaltered most of the elements of this episode, which is the keystone of both his poem's structure and its theme, many of the circumstantial details that seem to corroborate his interpretation so effectively he either invented or obtained by distorting his original material. And since without these details his tone of conviction would often seem willfully capricious, it depends for its full impact on the reader's confidence in exactly this fidelity to factual detail that a comparison with that original material shows that it does not have.

MME DEBACKER—ANNA DE BEAUPRÉ
(MME MULHAUSEN—CLARA DE MILLEFLEURS)

Considering how frequently its tone is one of jocular discursiveness, *Red Cotton Night-Cap Country* keeps a remarkably sharp and steady focus on its theme. Every detail relates to the contradiction in Mellerio's character, and the whole poem comes to center on the dramatic leap that resolves those contradictions. The figure of Mme Debacker, as she appears in the poem, provides a good illustration of Browning's concentration on the issues at stake in Mellerio's life, because there every trait in her character is made to con-

tribute to her role as a foil to Mellerio's wavering and conflicting loyalties. In Browning's hands she is overwhelming-
ly single-minded and self-centered. Like a grub whose only
mission in life is to become a butterfly, a grub who has been

> Born, bred with just one instinct,—that of growth,—
> Her quality was, caterpillar-like,
> To all-unerringly select a leaf
> And without intermission feed her fill. . . .

> (4.783–86)

Joining the cousins in condemning her as a complete hypocrite, Browning doubts that Mm Debacker herself believed at
all in the religious practices she participated in with
Mellerio:

> What
> She did believe in, I as little doubt,
> Was—[Anna's] self's own birthright to sustain
> Existence, grow from grub to butterfly,
> Upon unlimited [Mellerio]-leaf. . . .

> (4.844–48)[4]

Still, "Of the masks / That figure in this little history, / She
only has a claim to my respect" (4.740–42), and what Browning most respects in her is the strength of will with which she
pursued her goal, however "inferiorly proposed" (4.762) that
goal may have been. It is a familiar theme in Browning's
verse, dating back to "The Statue and the Bust" and beyond:
his admiration of anyone who has the courage of his conviction, no matter how warped—"Though the end in sight was
a vice, I say" ("The Statue and the Bust," l. 248). For
Browning, Mme Debacker serves two major thematic purposes: as an instance of calculated concentration of purpose,
in contrast to Mellerio's frantic indecision, and as an instance of a narrow and unscrupulous self-interest, in contrast to Mellerio's conflicting and generous affections.

When this rather sinister figure is compared with that
which emerges from the original documents, it appears that
in order to fit Mme Debacker into his theme Browning was
unfairly hard on her. In the documents the most striking impression Mme Debacker makes is of an aloof dignity, an im-

penetrability that even Mellerio remarked on in his famous letter to Dr. Pasquier of 10 August 1869, cited in the court's formal judgment: "Neither you, nor I, nor anyone sees into her heart" (p. 121). This sense of her remoteness may be the source of Browning's comment that, when he happened one day to come across Mme Debacker in person, she was so "colorless" and "featureless" that "The whole effect amounts with me to—blank! / I never saw what I could less describe" (1.842–47). But when he came to write the poem, he found something to describe by including as established facts many of the allegations made against her in the trial, even though not one of them was ever proved. The portrait of Mme Debacker offered by Browning in *Red Cotton Night-Cap Country* as an objective record is, in fact, to suit his own private purposes, largely a duplication of the caricature offered by the Mellerio heirs in the trial to suit their own private purposes.

For instance, in the trial it was undisputed that, before she met Mellerio, Mme Debacker had lived in London with her husband, an unsuccessful tailor, and had subsequently returned alone to Paris "because he would have exploited her beauty" (p. 40). But the heirs went on to allege that she then took up the career of a courtesan, being "first kept by a M. de Mongino" (p. 40), whom she left only when she found more tempting prey in Mellerio. This charge was then indignantly denied by Mme Debacker's attorney as an "outrageous . . . slander" (p. 66). The burden of proof would seem to lie with the heirs, but no evidence whatever was submitted on this point by either side—there was just the charge and then the flat denial. But although it was an entirely unsupported allegation, Browning retailed it as plain fact. He found the idea of Mme Debacker's prostitution doubly useful, as implying not only that she was willing to go to any extreme to provide luxurious comfort for herself but also that her husband's insult must have made her feel more affronted in "her rights / To wifely independence, then as wronged / Otherwise by the course of life proposed" (2.649–51), since on her return to Paris she is said to have adopted exactly the course she had repudiated. Thus, this blot on her character served to suggest both characteristics Browning wished her to display—independent willpower and calculated concern for self.

The next incident in which Mme Debacker's role in the poem differs significantly from her role in the original documents concerns the matter of her separation from her husband. In Browning's version it is quite simple: when M. Debacker became a fashionable and wealthy tailor, he wished to prevent his wife from claiming her share of her husband's income and so deposed his "complaint of wrong" (2.880) to obtain a decree of separation. Although the narration takes about eighty lines, the brunt of its emphasis is all on how embarrassing the whole affair was for Mellerio—a "splash / Into the mid-shame" (2.903–4), a "rough but wholesome shock" (2.827) undergone for Mme Debacker's sake. She herself is nearly absent, visible only as a cause of scandal and humiliation. But in the accounts of the trial, it is made clear that the reason for M. Debacker's action was that he had formed a liaison with a Mlle Viel, as Mme Debacker had with Mellerio, and he now wanted his way made legally clear to arranging a financial settlement with her (p. 53). Thus, morally he was as guilty as his wife; but in nineteenth-century France an adulterous husband could only be fined, and then only if he introduced his partner into the conjugal house, whereas an adulterous wife ran the risk of imprisonment. He was, in effect, blackmailing Mme Debacker into renouncing her share of her husband's new fortune by threatening her with charges of adultery. So actually she was something of a victim in this sordid affair, but in simplifying his account Browning omitted every circumstance that might possibly have created sympathy for her. Her attorney, for instance, pointed out that "there were more than 100,000 francs involved in this sacrifice, because M. Debacker was already in the full flush of prosperity. But she chose to stay with Antonio, whose father, mother, and brother were at that time all still alive. It certainly cannot have been greed that guided her" (p. 53). The remoteness of Mme Debacker's prospects of inheritance is obscured in Browning, where he implies that the (undated) episode concerning her husband occurred *after* the deaths of both Mellerio's father and his brother.

Then, in order to reinforce the idea that Mme Debacker's overriding concern throughout her life with Mellerio had been to protect her own source of sustenance, Browning gave the impression, through details that his original did not contain, that Mme Debacker herself was the indirect initiator of all Mellerio's many activities, keeping him harmlessly occupied through tasks "I used to busy you about, / And make believe you worked for my surprise!" (4.460–61). Even the elaborate restoration of the château is presented as work "I made you build, / And think an inspiration of your own" (4.457–58). Also, the heirs had unsuccessfully claimed that Mme Debacker dominated Mellerio completely, tyrannizing over him and forcing him to do her will; Browning was more subtle, but the effect is similar. He made Mme Debacker seem condescending, manipulative, and occasionally even sinister, as in the insistence that bequeathing Tailleville to the Convent of la Délivrande had been originally her idea: "Hers was the instigation—none but she / . . . begged and prayed / That, when no longer she could supervise / The House, it should become a Hospital" (1.805, 814–16). This insinuation is of a piece with the heirs' allegation that Mme Debacker callously exploited Mellerio's religious sentiments, "us[ing] the name of a Convent of holy maidens . . . to gain control over Antonio for her own profit and to disguise and protect the testament by the inclusion of respectable legatees who thus would also find themselves interested parties" (p. 90). This allegation was rejected—there was not even any evidence submitted to support it—but Browning included it anyway, with all its implications of calculated hypocrisy on Mme Debacker's part, and then presumed to "praise / Her forethought which prevented leafless stalk / Bestowing any hoarded succulence" (4.852–54) on the undeserving cousins.

Two other incidents in the poem that imply Mme Debacker's brazen acquisitiveness were also fabricated. They are both highly dramatic, and therefore appealing to a dramatic poet, but neither can actually have occurred. The first concerns Mme Debacker's alleged crow of triumph—"I have him!"—on being reconciled to Mellerio after the mutilation of his hands. The heirs contended that Mme Debacker leaped into Mellerio's carriage as he was leaving a relative's home one day and carried him off. The next day, they continued, Mellerio brought Morel, the faithful family agent, to Mme Debacker's house to be told about the pair's new plans, and Mme Debacker was said to have sneered at the annuity the family had earlier offered her as a settlement, crying, "I have him!" (*Je le tiens!*" [p. 45]). In rebuttal the defense labeled the entire episode a "fiction" (p. 65), claiming that Mellerio had independently appeared one day at Mme Debacker's house, and pointed out in support of their defense that if Mme Debacker actually had been so vindictive, "if Morel had heard any such thing, he would hardly have sent her his compliments in a letter to Antonio a few days later" (p. 66). The court, in its judgment, found this alleged remark of Mme Debacker's to be *"completely implausible"* (p. 124), because none of the plaintiffs "could explain why [Morel], who should have been outraged by her disgraceful remark, then asked in his letters to Antonio that his appreciation be forwarded to Anna for her devoted care, and sent her his best regards" (p. 124). Nevertheless, Browning included the speech verbatim, without any hint of its dubious authenticity, and even enlarged the putative audience from one single servant to the entire assembled family, so that the implausible gesture of defiance became a ceremonial declaration of war.

The other incident that Browning provided to display Mme Debacker's strength of will is her climactic tirade following Mellerio's death. This long speech, together with Browning's interpretative reaction, is the last major section of the poem, followed only by one hundred lines of quick conclusion. In this scene Mme Debacker faces the cousins, who have come to claim their inheritance, and reveals to them that Mellerio has left everything to la Délivrande, with a life-interest for herself. Finally, as "laugh grew frown, and frown grew terrible" (4.683), "shriek[ing]" (4.684) "Vituper-ative[ly]" (4.716), she ends by denouncing the cousins' selfish hypocrisy. This explosive culmination is Mme Debacker's only occasion of self-defense in the poem, and although Browning's subsequent commentary on her gradually cools, he does at this point approve of her as she "stands in pride of place" (4.737). But although a good deal of what Mme Debacker says was paraphrased from her attorney's arguments in the accounts of the trial, the circumstances of the event as Browning so dramatically pictured it are far from the literal truth: what actually happened, when the cousins confronted Mme Debacker after Mellerio's death, was a prolonged negotiation, "which aimed at the avoidance of the [imminent] lawsuit by mutual concession" (p. 122). Mme Debacker signed a document acknowledging "some acts of eccentricity on Antonio's part" (p. 49), and in return she was offered a life estate in Tailleville plus an annuity of 12,000 francs. She demanded 15,000 francs, which the heirs at first refused, but they later grew anxious enough to consent to a subsequent demand for 18,000. Thus, the case would never have come to trial at all if M. Debacker, who was legally required to authorize his wife's litigation, had then not refused to agree to an annuity of less than 25,000 francs for her (p. 49). So the case finally did go to court, but only after this prolonged series of negotiations, which hardly suggests the staunchly righteous confidence Mme Debacker was made to display in the inflammatory scene that Browning invented for her in his poem.

On the whole, Browning's attitude toward Mme Debacker as she appears in *Red Cotton Night-Cap Country* is a curious mixture of distaste for her unconventional sexual morality and admiration for her strong-minded independence. The attitudes are familiar ones to students of Browning: his relationship with Elizabeth Barrett is only the most prominent example of his tendency to prudish passivity where women were concerned, and in his poetry Pompilia is only the most obvious instance of his adoration of ideal strength and purity of character. In Mme Debacker's case, his insistent excuse for dwelling at such length on her flaws of character is that, after all, the material is a matter of public record:

> Would I re-tell this story of your woes,
> Would I have heart to do you detriment
> By pinning all this shame and sorrow plain
> To that poor *chignon* . . .
>
> . . . .
>
> But that men read it, rough in brutal print,

As two years since some functionary's voice
Rattled all this—and more by every much—
Into the ear of vulgar Court and crowd?

(2.681–89)

But as with Mellerio himself, the traits that Browning apparently wished Mme Debacker to present most clearly cannot be found, in anything like the clarity he suggests, in the historical documents from which he so often professes to be drawing them.

NOTRE DAME DE LA DÉLIVRANDE (THE RAVISSANTE)

The third and last topic to be considered here is the role played in this poem by the institutions—the church and, to a lesser degree, the law. In his admiration of the individual who single-mindedly pursues his own truth as he sees it, Browning, like his early idol Shelley before him, consistently disparaged a weak reliance on convention, reserving an especially fierce disdain for social structures that have compromised an original impulse of idealism by becoming complacent bastions of the status quo. In *The Ring and the Book*, the judgments of the various officials of the church and the court are so distorted by myopia and selfish interest that they actually contribute to the catastrophe by their inability to transcend a petty insistence on conventional regulation. Only the saintly Pope has both the insight to perceive the subtle truths that elude the institutional machinery and the integrity to act decisively on that insight without concern for his personal advantage. In *Red Cotton Night-Cap Country* Browning once again set out to re-create a historical event that would display in life one of his favorite literary themes—the various modes of inadequacy in institutionalized approaches to the truths of spiritual life.

The church in this poem is again the Roman Catholic church, represented this time by the Convent of Notre Dame de la Charité des Orphelines de Marie de la Délivrande, familiarly known as either la Vierge-Fidèle (the Faithful Virgin) or la Délivrande. This convent was, and still is, primarily an orphanage, remotely connected with the Missionary Fathers of la Délivrande. (For an account of the founding of the orphanage, see pp. 68–69.) Mellerio had been involved to some degree with the Missionary Fathers, but he had left the legacy to the convent; and the religious organizational structure was loose enough that the Missionary Fathers were not involved in the suit. The name "la Délivrande" must have been a difficult problem for Browning when he decided to change all the original names to avoid a libel suit. "La Délivrande" is popularly supposed to be associated with *la délivrance* ("rescue"), whereas actually, according to a little pamphlet recently published by the convent, it is a distortion of *la Delle Yvrande*, an ancient name for the region derived etymologically from the Saxon *delle* ("valley," English "dale") and the Celtic *ewi-randa* ("water"-"frontier"): "the valley where water marks the frontier."[5] In Roman times the Delle Yvrande was the valley of the small Douvette River, which served as the boundary between the two Gallic tribes of the Baiocasses and the Viducasses. But over the centuries popular superstition had transformed this meaning to "the Deliveress," and Browning had found this confusion very useful to demonstrate Mellerio's gullibility:

> This Ravissante, now: when he saw the church
> For the first time, and to his dying-day,
> His firm belief was that the name fell fit
> From the Delivering Virgin, niched and known;
> As if there wanted records to attest
> The appellation was a pleasantry,
> A pious rendering of Rare Vissante,
> The proper name which erst our province bore.
>
> (2.152–59)

When Browning changed "la Délivrande" to "la Ravissante," he gained a nice suggestion of a rather violent power of fascination, but he lost all etymological connection with "Delivering Virgin."

The darker connotation of Browning's choice of name for the convent is only a small part of his systematic denigration of its role in Mellerio's drama. In Mellerio himself, Browning subordinated all else to show a dim but well-intentioned man trapped in a painful dilemma. It is useful, almost necessary, for Browning that neither horn of this particular dilemma be really worth the suffering Mellerio undergoes in his inability to choose between them, because the point of the situation as Browning shows it is that the reality of Mellerio's suffering and the courage of his solution do not depend in any way on the inherent value of the alternatives between which his choice must be made. Mellerio is wavering not between an ideal romantic love and an ideal religious faith but between Mme Debacker and the Convent of la Délivrande. So, for the same reasons that Browning presented Mme Debacker in the poem as a specimen "inferiorly proposed" (4.762), a grade of "pettier love" (4.867), regardless of her actual role in the real event, he also lost no opportunity in the poem to show the convent as grasping, ruthless, and conniving, in spite of the fact that there was such an utter lack of evidence to support the plaintiffs' charges concerning the convent that they were shamed into dropping all of them right in the middle of the suit.

The dominant trait in Browning's portrait of the convent is greed. First summoned to Tailleville by a tortured Mellerio "for the cure of soul-disease" (3.865), the "none-excluding, all-collecting Church" (1.965) is depicted as being content to depart with "palm well crossed with coin" (3.952) rather than insisting on the fact of sin and refusing to let Mellerio think he could bribe his way to forgiveness. There is a parallel here between Browning's disapproval of the convent's self-serving leniency and his disapproval of Mme Debacker's protection of Mellerio, as she consistently chose to "smoothen truth away" (4.863) rather than force him to the painful choice. Still, Browning sees extenuating circumstances in Mme Debacker's case that he cannot find in the convent's, and his censure becomes scatological as he contemplates the

> Father Priest
> And Mother Nun, who came and went and came,
> Beset this [Tailleville], trundled money-muck
> To midden and the main heap oft enough. . . .
>
> (4.878–81)

Calling la Délivrande a dunghill is indeed graphic scorn for such greedy "posting" (3.864) to Tailleville for gifts time and time again, but Browning's heady indignation ignores the simple fact that the charge is clearly and utterly false. As their counsel pointed out, its inhabitants were cloistered, so none of them could ever have come to the château at any time, for any purpose (p. 79). There was not even any correspondence between the convent and Mellerio, except for "one circular for lottery tickets and, five months after the testament, two banal letters concerning [assistance in obtaining a domestic servant,] a service which M. Mellerio also requested from his cousin Mme Agnel and which events did not permit to be rendered" (p. 79). However delighted the convent may actually have been to receive benefactions, there was really no evidence whatever that it actively sought them, let alone that such scheming was its only motive for its dealings with Mellerio.

But in *Red Cotton Night-Cap Country*, the image of the convent is entirely one of a self-serving materialism, whose only interest lies in exploiting the credulity of the faithful for its own worldly advantage. Browning calls such corrupt religion a "superstition," "extinct . . . with my good will" (4.887–88); but to understand his position, it is necessary to recall that his own religious convictions were very strong, and that he is contemptuous of the kind of practices he portrays in his poem exactly because he sees them as so rank a travesty of the true spiritual teaching Mellerio so badly needed. Browning judges Mellerio's faith in such miracle-mongering to have been admirably deep and sincere, but sadly misdirected—"sickly," "foolish and fantastic" (3.851,937). It is another instance of separating a judgment of the quality of a man's commitment from a judgment of the merit of the object his commitment seizes on. As Mellerio had failed to perceive the inferior nature of his relations with Mme Debacker,

> So with his other instance of mistake;
> Was Christianity the [Délivrande]?
>
> (2.470–71)

Browning is finally so disgusted by the grossness of this superstition from which, in his opinion, all spiritual life has been drained, that, in what is perhaps the most grotesque passage of the entire poem, he dismisses it as nothing but the

corpse of real Christianity, and imagines drawing a heavy
night-cap

> O'er such a decomposing face of things,
> Once so alive, it seemed immortal too!
>
> (4.892–93)

With both Mellerio's mistress and his religion, then,
Browning has gone to some pains to ensure that they are
both perceived as unworthy of his devotion, so that a sharp
contrast is created between the moral and the intellectual di-
mensions of Mellerio's quandary, and hence between the
positive extreme of Mellerio's moral courage and the negative extreme of his intellectual obtuseness. "The heart was
wise according to its lights / And limits" (4.757–58); but if
Mellerio had only "exerted brain" (4.745), he would have
discerned the inadequacy of Mme Debacker's overprotective
love. He would also have built up

> some better theory
> Of how God operates in heaven and earth,
> Than would establish Him participant
> In doings yonder at the [Délivrande].
>
> (4.753–56)

It was this interest in showing the two claimants to Mellerio's affection at their worst that seems to me the most proba-
ble source for Browning's most blatant departure of all from
the objective fact he claims to be retailing so faithfully—his
entire omission of the major portion of the lawsuit, the portion dealing with the charges of undue influence against
Mme Debacker and the convent. In the poem the only legal
issue is "to dispute / [Antonio Mellerio's] competence, / Being insane, to make a valid will" (4.896–98). No mention is
even made of the other half of the charges, or of the fact that
the convent was also a party to the suit. Clearly, Browning's
dark insinuations concerning Mme Debacker and the convent would not have been well served by an obligation to
admit that all charges against both were found to be totally
without foundation, and that they both were totally exoner-
ated.

The convent's innocence, in particular, as has been mentioned, was brilliantly vindicated by their demonstration of

such an entire lack of evidence that the heirs were forced to make a public retraction of the charges in the middle of the suit (see pp. 88–89, 91). Simply ignoring this dimension of the case had several advantages for Browning: it avoided an inconveniently positive impression of the convent and the mistress, it helped keep the focus of the poem's attention directed on the mental condition of Mellerio himself, and it obviated the need for a full explanation of the complicated issues involved in the court's handling of the case.

This last point is significant. In the poem Browning summarizes the court's judgment in forty-four quoted lines, mentioning that the family had, after all, found Mellerio to be quite sane enough to do business with, then declaring his religious eccentricities to have been " 'Neither excessive nor inordinate' " (4.947), and finally deciding that his death was an " 'accident / Which ended fatally. The case is closed' " (4.954–55). Not only does this manner of presentation perpetuate the illusion that the question of suicide was as central an issue in fact as it was made to be in the poem, but the tone of brisk self-confidence in this passage is an important contribution to the impression Browning created for the court in his poem. That impression is one of a straightforward, rather plodding institutionalized competency, one that dealt fairly with the most obvious facts of the case but that was not capable of probing beneath the surface to the deeper truths available only to intuition. In much the same way that Browning showed in *The Ring and the Book* the Roman court finding Guido Franceschini guilty without ever understanding the real motives involved, so here he shows the French court reaching the correct verdict regarding Mellerio's sanity without even glimpsing the underlying reality—as Browning sees it—of his behavior. Although the judges do not even dimly perceive what Browning takes to be the real meaning of Mellerio's death, their judgment, "issued with all regularity, [was] just, inevitable, / Nowise to be contested by what few / Can judge the judges" (4.908–11). But in spite of the poem's impression of a merely superficial accuracy in the court's performance, the legal documents, especially the disinterested summary of the public prosecutor and the text of the court's judgment, do in fact display a remarkably subtle sensitivity to each issue of this complicated case. Furthermore, as has been demonstrated, to shore up his own imaginative interpretation of Mellerio's death, Browning altered or omitted so many corroborative facts that the cumulative effect of reading the trial transcripts is remarkably different from that of reading the poem.

On the whole, I think it is probably fair to say that it would really not have been possible for Browning to make a convincing case for his conclusions by attempting to derive them from the facts exactly as they appeared in the actual event. Such an extreme statement concerning the discrepancy between the poem and its sources could not be made about *The Ring and the Book*, where no single departure from the original sources is critical to the poem's general meaning; nor do those departures, even if taken all together, comprise as radical a transformation of that material as occurs in *Red Cotton Night-Cap Country*. The real problem for Browning in this later poem, baldly stated, was that his two most important themes entailed mutually contradictory treatments of his source material. On the one hand, to stress the possibility of using the imagination to perceive truths veiled beneath the vulgar facts "reported in the newspaper" (4.31) required him to demonstrate a carefully maintained fidelity to literal detail; but, on the other, to find in those facts a pattern of evolving moral education leading inevitably to moral action required a degree of adjustment of those facts that was inconstent with literal fidelity. The facts simply did not fit both themes, and what was sacrificed to fit both themes into the poem was a kind of integrity in its claim to literal historical truth. This sacrifice is not apparent within the work itself; indeed, there it is carefully obscured. But when the poem is examined in relation to its sources, *Red Cotton Night-Cap Country* gives the impression that here Browning sought to exploit all the thematic advantages of the kind of factual basis he had so successfully used in *The Ring and the Book*, without being willing to forgo interpretations that were not really supported by that factual basis.

There are interesting comparisons to be made, on this subject of the relationship between a work and its sources, between *Red Cotton Night-Cap Country* and the other poems of similar scale that followed it in the last sixteen years of Browning's career. Out of the last twelve volumes he published, only four are comparably large: *Aristophanes' Apology* (1875), *The Inn Album* (1875), *The Agamemnon of Aeschylus* (1877), and *Parleyings with Certain People of Importance in Their Day* (1887). In none of these did Browning engage in quite the same sort of effort to display the profound psychology hidden under historical evidence as he had in *The Ring and the Book* and *Red Cotton Night-Cap Country*, although all four of the later poems were based, to one degree or another, on objective fact that easily could have lent itself to such treatment.

Aristophanes' Apology consists of an elaborately convoluted dramatic monologue framing a translation of Euripides' *Herakles*. Browning scrupulously kept this frame separate from the drama for which it provides such a startling foil, a treatment that is in marked contrast to his earlier handling of Euripides' *Alkestis* in *Balaustion's Adventure* (1871). There the narrator's recital of the play—part direct translation, part summary—has a quasi-Christian interpretation that is thoroughly interwoven with her own dramatic situation and is only tenuously related to the original play that the poem purports to reproduce. The method of *Red Cotton Night-Cap Country*, in fact, closely resembles that of *Balaustion's Adventure*, since both poems depend heavily on giving the impression that what is in fact a very loose "translation" is faithfully close to the original. Two years after *Red Cotton Night-Cap Country*, however, in *Aristophanes' Apology*, his second dramatic recital, Browning entirely avoided the disingenuousness which that earlier method required. It is an interesting speculation that perhaps his experience with *Red Cotton Night-Cap Country* contributed to his change of approach. As for *The Agememnon of Aeschylus*, published two years after *Aristophanes' Apology*, that is nothing more than a painfully literal translation, "literal at every cost save that of absolute violence to our language," as Browning boasted in his "Preface."[6] In that work he made no gesture at all toward interpreting the raw material of the original play.

Although *The Inn Album*, like *Red Cotton Night-Cap*

Country, was based on historical events, "an actual occurrence in the life of Lord de Ros (1792–1839),"[7] the poem stands at such a far remove from those events that it derives no particular thematic impact from that circumstance. It has no significant connection with its source, and makes no claim whatever to specific historical factuality. It might as well be completely fictional. In Browning's last major poem, *Parleyings*, which traces the influence of seven moral and aesthetic figures on his own early development, he did return to a mode whose appreciation obviously requires a recognition of its intimate relation to extrinsic material, but in this case the poem is so frankly subjective that its real connection is not so much to the works of those seven men as to Browning's own idiosyncratic interpretations of them. The accuracy of those interpretations is not really a central issue. Consequently, for instance, William DeVane's discovery that Browning had radically misrepresented Bernard de Mandeville, the subject of the first parleying, is really more of an interesting curiosity than a revaluation of Browning's method, since the themes of the parleyings do not fundamentally depend on whether or not the portraits they present are good likenesses.[8] So, in spite of the fact that Browning's later poetry, even more than his earlier, came to stress the practical consequences of moral decisions, *Red Cotton Night-Cap Country* was the last long poem in which he sought to demonstrate that principle at work in the public records of an actual life. Comparison of the poem with those public records raises the question as to whether his abandonment of this technique may have been related to an increasing impatience with the recalcitrance of "pure crude fact" as a sufficiently transparent manifestation of the themes he asked it to display. For all his reputation of being oblivious to aesthetic subtleties—a reputation that he acknowledged in the Young Man's jibe in *The Inn Album*, "That bard's a Browning; he neglects the form: / But ah, the sense, ye gods, the weighty sense!" (1.17–18)—a study of the sources of *Red Cotton Night-Cap Country* suggests the poet's dissatisfaction with the failure of a complex set of objective facts to shape themselves into as clear and elegant an illustration of a desired set of themes as he could have wished. At any rate, never again did Browning embark on such a project.

6

Later Developments

Maître Carel, counsel for the convent in the 1872 trial, was not only indulging in courtroom rhetoric when he remarked that the Mellerio heirs were not given to hanging back where their financial interests were concerned. Undaunted by the judgment brought so resoundingly against them, they immediately took their case to the Cour d'Appel de Caen; and when that appeal was denied in 1873, they turned in 1874 for one last effort to the Cour de Cassation, the highest court of appeal in France available for this sort of civil matter. Only when the highest court refused to see merit in their case did they abandon their efforts to take possession of their cousin's estate. This chapter presents highlights of the documents relating to those developments that occurred after 23 January 1873, the date Browning finished writing his poem. Although these documents obviously do not provide direct insight into Browning's transformation of history into poetry, they do often clarify obscurities in that history, and also give many interesting glimpses into further aspects of it for those readers who may have become curious as to its final resolution.

We know that Browning himself was aware of the 1873 appeal. In a letter to Miss Annie Egerton Smith, dated 3 August 1873, he remarked, "It appears that the Cousins appealed, and tried their luck once again, and, only a week ago, were again signally beaten as they deserved. I am to see the newspaper report" (*Letters of Robert Browning*, ed. Hood, p. 158). Since the Meynell Collection of the Armstrong Browning Library at Baylor University does contain the account of the 1873 appeal published in the *Journal de Caen*, presumably Browning did learn something of the details of this first appeal; but there is no evidence suggesting that he ever saw the official court documents—the briefs and the decisions—from which selections are given below. (A trial has "pleadings" and a "judgment"; an appeal has "briefs" and a "decision.") Their appearance here thus marks the first connection made between them and *Red Cotton Night-Cap Country*. Since for obvious reasons these appeals involve a great deal of repetition of material from the original trial, I have provided a summary narrative of the bulk of these documents, quoting directly only when they introduce either interesting new arguments or important new evidence. This chapter will first examine the briefs, the arguments, and the decision of the 1873 appeal, then glance at the 1874 appeal to the Cour de Cassation, and conclude with a personal view of the entire case written in 1893 by Joseph Mellerio, one of the original plaintiffs.

THE 1873 BRIEFS

The one hundred and nine allegations in the plaintiffs' 1873 brief contain, in one form or another, all but three of the sixty-three original 1872 allegations. Because charges of undue influence against the convent had been dropped in the course of the original trial, the three allegations relating to those charges (nos. 32–34 in the 1872 list) were omitted from the 1873 list; also, the summary allegation of 1872 (no. 63; in 1873 no. 106) was revised in 1873 to delete all reference to the convent. Otherwise, all the 1872 allegations reappear in 1873, largely unaltered except for a consistent effort to improve the precision of dating in those allegations dealing with Mellerio's unsoundness of mind, in order to satisfy the legal requirement that Mellerio be shown to have been insane at the exact periods of drawing up his testaments. The Court of Appeal, however, did not find the heirs' efforts in this regard to have been very convincing. Indeed, the public prosecutor found that the vagueness of dating where Mellerio's alleged acts of mental derangement were concerned continued to be so prevalent as to "suggest deliberate policy on the part of the heirs."

In general, the forty-six new allegations in 1873 are devoted to presenting further and far more bizarre examples of Mellerio's deranged behavior in the last few years of his life. The single most important exception to this generalization is number 55: "that the power wielded by Mme Debacker at that time (1869) was so great that she had successfully destroyed Antonio Mellerio's independence to the point of writing letters in his name, imitating his handwriting." This single vague and general suggestion of forgery is the only reference in the heirs' entire 1873 brief to the issues on which their appeal really depended: their new contention that Mellerio's last testaments were actually forgeries.

The difficulty for the heirs in bringing this charge lay in the legal procedural requirement that in appealing a judgment of the lower court an appellant is not permitted to introduce entirely new grounds of argument. New evidence may be brought in to support the original grounds; but if new grounds are introduced, then the process is no longer an appeal but an entirely new case, which is clearly not appropriate for consideration by an appellate court. In order to skirt this technicality, therefore, the Mellerio heirs did not file formal charges of forgery, but instead appended to their brief an "Explicatory Note" (not found in the archives, but referred to in some detail in the 1874 decision of the Cour de Cassation). Through this peculiar tactic they hoped to introduce material relevant to the issue of forgery without exactly violating the requirements of appellate court procedure. Both defendants, in their 1873 briefs, were especially concerned to have the court "disregard the alleged unrecognizability of handwriting here submitted for the first time by the Mellerio heirs, particularly since they have not formally pleaded this point." This procedural irregularity was a critical factor in the heirs' loss of both this and their subsequent appeal.

Other than the powder keg represented by number 55, the most interesting material added to the original 1872 list of the plaintiff's allegations is the recital of the following series of episodes, intended to demonstrate not only that Antonio Mellerio was, at least at intervals, completely unbalanced but that Mme Debacker was well aware of his unsoundness of mind and calculatedly exploited it:

> 58) that in August 1869 a former servant, who had been in the household for years, said to a priest who was acquainted with Antonio Mellerio, "That poor gentleman is becoming

more and more insane, so it is lucky that his madness has a religious bent";

59) that often Antonio Mellerio would go to visit this former servant, where he would help himself to whatever she had, whether farm animals or household goods, to perform deeds of charity at her expense;

60) that in the course of the year 1869, he ordered a hogshead of brandy and a cask of wine to be brought to the square in front of la Délivrande, for the pilgrims to refresh themselves;

61) that when the mayor of Douvres objected to this irregular arrangement, Antonio then offered the wine to several individuals, all of whom refused it, and he finally sent it to a clergyman, who accepted it;

62) that this act of distributing the brandy took place in the very square in front of la Délivrande, and that it was this publicity that brought about the intervention of the mayor;

. . .

67) that during the last months of 1869, Antonio Mellerio, in the company of Maître Hébert, who was then the notary at Douvres, had a meeting with another notary in the vicinity; that when they came to the business at hand he understood none of it, rambling so incoherently that on several occasions he had to be brought to his senses by Maître Hébert himself;

. . .

70) that one day during the last months of 1869 he had a fit of madness in the house of a woman named Nivel, to whom he had brought a horse blanket and a piece of flannel for curtains;

71) that, having presented the old woman with these gifts, he tried to confess her;

. . .

74) that one evening of the same year, 1869, he appeared at the house of a farmer living in Langrune who had a sick horse, asking to be shown the animal so that he might cure it;

75) that he then spent several hours in bizarre practices, pouring water and wine in the ears of this animal while reciting prayers;

76) that toward one o'clock in the morning, servants sent by Mme Debacker to find him arrived and tried to carry him home by force;

77) that he then went to the sheepfold, where he picked up a little lamb and carried it off in his arms;

78) that he returned a few minutes later to ask the master of the house to send the shepherd and the flock of sheep over to Tailleville the next day, because he wanted to have dinner for them at the château;

79) that on the next day the shepherd, and the flock, found what amounted to a feast prepared for them;

80) that Antonio then said to the shepherd, "I took the little lamb to bed with me, but I got covered with insects and parasites; I had it take a bath of purification and now it is the 'Agnus Dei' ";

81) that from that time on he frequently bathed with his little lamb in his bath of purification;

82) that, returning one day to the shepherd, be begged him to come to Tailleville with his flock of sheep from time to time to keep the "Agnus Dei" company, for fear that it was becoming bored all by itself;

83) that when the horse so peculiarly tended by Antonio Mellerio died, he sent another from his own stables to replace the one the farmer had lost;

84) that Mme Debacker sent a servant to repossess the horse, on the grounds that Antonio was mad and could not possibly have understood how irrational it was to make such a gift;

85) that, still during the same period of 1869, Antonio arranged for a billy goat to be harnessed to a specially made carriage, in which he had himself driven around the park;

86) that one day when the animal did not want to move, Antonio said to it, "All right, if you don't want to pull me, you must be pulled yourself"; that he then had the goat forcibly placed in the carriage and driven around the park by some masons who were working on the château, while Antonio followed along behind, delighted with the scene;

87) that while the remodeling of Tailleville was being finished, in 1869, on the pretext that the dove was the bird of God and that the pigeon partook of its nature, he decided that the pigeon house should be located above the chapel of the château, and gave orders to the carpenter for it to be constructed there. But Mme Debacker told the carpenter to stay away from the château for a few days, saying that Antonio would quickly forget this insane plan. Indeed, by the time the carpenter returned, Antonio no longer remembered it;

88) that toward the middle of 1869, he often went to Langrune to visit a dirty and repulsive old woman named Marotte, for whom he showed great affection;

89) that one day, passing by a house whose door was open, he climbed through the window, took two pillows that he found on the bed, and carried them to Marotte;

90) that, one day in the same year, he took a worthless little plaster virgin from the house of this same Marotte and carried it ceremoniously through the whole village, to enshrine it, he said, in the place of honor in his chapel, a dignity that it deserved because it belonged to Marotte;

91) that on another day he came from Tailleville bringing

157

Marotte a piece of bread on a silver tray, with an ornate and elegant carafe full of wine;

92) that he presented the silver tray and the carafe to a neighbor of Marotte's, on the pretext that she had once wished to give him a piece of bread for the Vinde woman;

93) that the next day Mme Debacker sent to have the objects returned, offering a cash compensation;

94) that in this same year, 1869, Antonio Mellerio came to a neighboring priest, asking permission to play music in his church; the priest consented, remarking to the sacristan, "Let him do it, he's not in his right mind";

95) that Antonio began banging on the organ with all his might and chanting at the top of his voice, making such a racket that the inhabitants of the village rushed to the church;

96) that the sacristan, who was present, could not restrain his hilarity at Antonio Mellerio's grimaces;

97) that he once went to a little village far from Tailleville expressly to give alms to the poor, found the priest, conversed with the servant about epistles, evangels, and apostles, and forced the priest to take his entire wallet, in which the priest was later astonished to find only ten francs;

98) that he proposed to buy a house owned by a man in Langrune, who was renting it to old Marotte for forty francs a year, in order for her to establish a hospital there;

99) that, on being refused by the landowner, he said, "Then I will buy the house that you yourself are renting for your own occupancy, and give it to you as a gift";

100) that in October 1869 he brought to an inhabitant of Langrune who had a chest ailment a bunch of grapes, which he fed him one by one, reciting an "Ave" between each grape, adding that these grapes had a special power because the gloves with which he was serving them had been placed *ex voto* in his chapel;

101) that when one of his workmen told him that his daughter was miserably poor, he went to this woman's house, minutely examined everything in it, even the interior of the bed, and ordered the workmen who had accompanied him to give her alms;

102) that during the last days of January 1870, he asked someone at la Délivrande to come sing in his chapel while he himself, Mellerio, said mass;

. . .

107) that often this pressure by Mme Debacker was so great that he wished to be free of her at any cost;

108) that he went to the Commissioner of Police of la Délivrande to beg him to make Mme Debacker leave the château, offering to give him 25,000 francs if he succeeded in

having her sent to New Caledonia; [The French took control of this Pacific archipelago in 1853, and had begun to use it as a penal colony in 1864, only some four or five years before this alleged pathetic request.]

109) that another Commissioner of Police in the neighborhood, during 1868 and 1869, was the witness of scenes of madness on the part of Antonio Mellerio and of the power exerted over him by Mme Debacker;

Mme Debacker, in her brief, requested the court to disregard entirely this new list of allegations, "rejecting it as improbable, immaterial, and inadmissible as demonstrated by the evidence of the case." She particularly requested the court to disregard "the Explicatory Note of the appellants with respect to the handwriting and signature of the testament of M. Antonio Mellerio, declaring that the Explicatory Note does not state a claim upon which relief can be founded" (since it is not in fact a formal allegation). The convent also appeared in the 1873 appeal as a codefendant because, even though during the course of the original trial the heirs had been forced to drop all charges against them, they still ran the risk of being deprived of their inheritance if the heirs succeeded in proving either that Mellerio was of unsound mind or that the disputed testaments were forgeries. Consequently in their brief the convent asked the court "to confirm the formal withdrawal by the Mellerio heirs of all charges of exercise of undue influence made against the Convent," to disregard the new list of allegations, and especially "to disregard the alleged unrecognizability of handwriting here submitted to the Court for the first time by the Mellerio heirs, particularly since they have not formally pleaded this point; and to declare this charge to be inadmissible as being tardy, irresponsible [abandonnée], incompatible with the nature of the grounds of the suit, and consequently not properly part of this case."

THE 1873 APPEAL

The 1873 appeal lasted from 8 July to 28 July, involving five days of argument and one of the court's announcement of its decision. As in the trial, attorneys for the heirs, for Mme Debacker, and for the convent presented their arguments in turn. Since there was no rebuttal, their statements were

159

followed immediately by that of the public prosecutor. (In courts of appeal the title of this official is *procureur général* rather than *procureur de la République*, but because his function remains the same I have retained the same translation.) Although the account given below, taken from the issues of the *Journal de Caen* on file in the Meynell Collection of the Browning Armstrong Library at Baylor University, does not provide as detailed a narrative of the 1873 appeal as *L'Ordre et la Liberté* did of the 1872 trial, it does make possible a clear understanding of the new developments of the case. *L'Ordre et la Liberté* in 1873 contented itself with a minimal summary of the case; its usefulness is eclipsed by the fuller version given in the *Journal de Caen.* There are no significant discrepancies.

Unfortunately, because they must have been exceedingly ingenious, the *Journal de Caen* did not report in much detail Maître Allou's arguments on behalf of the heirs concerning the procedural difficulties involved in their device of the Explicatory Note. It merely remarked that he "sought to establish that legally the charges that the testaments were forgeries cannot be rejected by estoppel," that is, by barring a party from making an allegation because his own previous action implies the contrary—in this instance, because suing for nullification of the testaments in the original trial implied a recognition that those testaments were in fact the work of Antonio Mellerio. Then, after submitting expert testimony from two handwriting analysts, M. des Radrets of Paris and M. Guilbert of Caen, Maître Allou concluded "that it is at least doubtful that the testaments were the work of M. Mellerio."

The heirs' accusation of forgery was aimed not only at the texts of the testaments themselves but also at the crucial letter from Mellerio to M. Prevost of 10 August 1869, in which he responded to the reproaches the notary had made to him on the subject of his intended bequests and defended his choice of Mme Debacker and the crippled poor as his beneficiaries. In fact, it was to discredit this damaging letter that the charges of forgery were brought in the first place; but this last-ditch tactic involved the heirs in all manner of embarrassing logical corollaries, since so many other documents submitted in the case, including the last testaments, were written in the same handwriting. The heirs were thus reduced to arguing, for instance, that it was the forger who wrote the original letter inviting M. Prevost to come visit Tailleville to give his advice concerning a proposed draft of the testament, a charge which implied that though Mellerio had not wished such a visit, nevertheless the forger had insisted. This is hardly plausible strategy for a person who presumably would have preferred her alleged campaign of undue influence to proceed undisturbed. The various counsels for the defense were skillful at exposing the absurdity— and the scurrility—of such charges. In particular, Maître Jouen, the special counsel Mme Debacker had retained to deal specifically with the charges of forgery, was so effective that he was complimented by the *Journal de Caen* reporter:

Maître Jouen, charged with defending the interests of Mme Debacker in the matter of forgery, has developed his case with remarkable skill, from both a substantive and a procedural point of view.

He maintains that neither *de facto* nor *de jure* [neither substantively nor procedurally] has any charge of forgery actually been brought by the Mellerio heirs, since they made no formal allegations on these grounds, and since consideration of this point cannot therefore be introduced before the Court. He also maintains that the heirs are estopped, according to Articles 464 and 214 of the Code of Civil Procedure, and that the Mellerio heirs, not having thought of this tactic in the original trial and not having then even intended later to impugn the handwriting of the testament, cannot now bring up this issue for the first time before this Court, because such a charge would constitute not merely additional evidence but an entirely different claim.

Turning to the evidence the Mellerio heirs have submitted in their efforts to impugn the handwriting of the testament, Maître Jouen first considers the testimony of the two experts, M. des Radrets and M. Guilbert. He demonstrates both the inconsistencies in their testimony and the maneuvers of the Mellerio heirs, who, in order to achieve the results they desired, were not content merely to confine the experts to inspecting only Mellerio's less well-written papers and signatures, holding back all examples of his normal handwriting because those did clearly resemble the handwriting of the testaments, but even went so far as to delete the doubts expressed in the professional opinion of M. des Radrets, in order to give the Court the impression of an absolute certitude on his part; but they neglected to secure his authorization for the version of his testimony that they submitted as evidence. When they were later required to obtain that authorization, the expert did not refuse to give it; but it is still obvious to anyone, declares Maître Jouen, that the deletions in the expert's opinion were not made by the expert. And he is astonished to find the Mellerio heirs complaining so loudly about forgery on the part of Mme Debacker, when they must for their own part account for this expertise so strangely riddled with deletions.

As for the expert testimony of M. Guilbert, Maître Jouen demonstrates that it is full of contradictions, such as having papers given the expert as models being themselves later judged to be highly suspect. In fact, one document declared by M. des Radrets to be the very model of Mellerio's handwriting was declared by M. Guilbert to be definitely not the work of Mellerio. . . .

Maître Jouen then proceeds to technical details concerning the formation of various individual letters, which, according to him, are the work of Mellerio in every case.

He shows how the heirs, in order to impugn the handwriting of one single document, have been forced by logic to impugn everything Mellerio wrote, not only in his actual correspondence but even in his notebook of first drafts, which has been submitted to the Court. Consequently, since that notebook also contains letters written to merchants and pharmacists, on insignificant subjects, the heirs' line of argument forces them to draw the conclusion that forgery was practiced even there—that is to say, purely for love of the art.

And that is not all! According to one of the experts, one of Mellerio's signatures is partly the work of Mellerio, and partly the work of a forger. Is that clear? Mellerio is said to have made one letter, the forger made the next, and so on, in turn, right down to the flourish.

When a suit has been reduced to such arguments as this, suggests Maître Jouen, it is desperate indeed.

Maître Jouen finishes his remarks by asking the Court to recognize the testaments as being written by Mellerio himself, and to allow itself to be guided in the other issues of the case by Maître Paris [Mme Debacker's chief counsel in the 1873 appeal].

After the presentation of arguments by all the various attorneys, this case, like the original trial, concluded with a statement from the public prosecutor, here a M. Delise, authoritatively weighing the merits of the case before submitting it to the judges for a decision. These remarks of M. Delise, like those of his counterpart in the original trial, are strikingly impressive for the clarity with which they isolate the essential legal issues and the pungency with which they approve or dispose of the various efforts resorted to by the advocates to promote their several causes.

Having commented that the case is an unusually important one, "both on account of the huge sums at stake and on account of certain extraordinary circumstances in Mellerio's life," M. Delise begins his impartial review of the evidence by remarking that though the heirs have systematically "distorted and biased" their account of Mellerio's early life in Parisian high society, it does nevertheless seem to be true that he "did participate in the sort of life to which, twenty years later, so many labels have been applied, and which is characterized mainly by an enormous vanity, an absence of all moral restraint, an unbounded appetite for pleasure, and an ostentatious parading of vice." But even so, with all its faults, such a life is hardly the "erotic delirium" that it appears to be in the heirs' version of it; and in fact, the public prosecutor concludes, with regard to the issues of the case the heirs' "investigation into Mellerio's youth has been irrelevant." As for their highly colored story of Mellerio's involvement with Mme Debacker, "the purity of whose morals he does not wish to defend," M. Delise merely remarks that though at first "she told Mellerio the usual tale [*le petit roman d'habitude*] very imaginatively, and he believed it all without hesitation," nevertheless subsequently "a deep and sincere affection sprang up between them that would endure the rest of their lives."

Coming to events touching more nearly on the case, M. Delise dismisses the heirs' allegation of Mellerio's madness following the cold bath of October 1867, because in any event "his recovery was prompt and complete, and it would be ungracious of the Mellerio heirs to contest this fact, since they have submitted a testament made by Mellerio in their favor the following March."

As for the death of his mother on 11 January 1868 "from an acute attack of apoplexy," M. Delise stresses that the main

163

reason that Mellerio's "profound despair mixed with contrition" on that occasion led to the appalling mutilation of his hands was that "although he sorely needed consolation, he was given none. . . . The priest and two nuns keeping vigil in the death chamber ruthlessly took advantage of his condition, immediately making him confess his sins and swear on his mother's body never to see Mme Debacker again. The conduct of the family was no more sympathetic. At the height of his grief, they spoke only of financial affairs." But even so, according to M. Delise, the documentary testimony from the period following this event is "important and decisive evidence, whose sources are Mellerio's friends, his doctors, and the heirs themselves," that Mellerio's weakened mind did in fact recover. "There can be no doubt on this question." M. Delise also completely dismisses the heirs' charges that Mme Debacker kidnapped Mellerio in her carriage, crying *"Je le tiens!"*: he remarks, "Also, at this time, Mellerio reestablished relations with Mme Debacker. It has been alleged that she brought pressure to bear on him, but it has been proved that he returned to her of his own free will as soon as he recovered his faculties."

Coming to a precise focus on the exact nature of the heirs' charge of Mellerio's unsoundness of mind and its interconnection with the charge of undue influence, M. Delise observes, "Without alleging absolute madness, the heirs maintain that after that time Mme Debacker continud to exert an influence over Mellerio's mind that he was not strong enough to resist." In response to this charge, M. Delise reviews Mme Debacker's "very convincing evidence" that Mellerio had fully recovered his mental balance, citing the tone of his correspondence, his insight into business affairs, and especially his repeated invitations to the family to visit him at Tailleville. "Mme Agnel came to stay for a holiday in the country, and she had the opportunity to see for herself if any kind of undue influence were being exerted. She observed the conditions there, and she continued to maintain affectionate relations with the household even after her departure."

The public prosecutor, turning to consider the documents submitted by the heirs on their behalf, begins to allow his personal opinion of them to appear more clearly. "One may well ask how the heirs could contest Antonio's testament in the face of such evidence. At a loss themselves, they have attempted to rely on one affidavit and one letter." These are the affidavit from Dr. Pasquier, quickly disposed of as being largely "opinions based only on information given second-hand to the doctor by the heirs and therefore worthless," and the letter from Jousse, "a travelling musician who was lodged and entertained for some time at the château of Tailleville, and who has hastened to repay that hospitality by accusing Mme Debacker of exerting undue influence. Such testimony, which may well be interested, is not to be trusted."

M. Delise then turns to examine one further document prominent in the appeal that had not been introduced in the original trial—the report filed by the local police after they had finished their own investigation into Mellerio's death. As a legal tactic, its introduction provided no advantage for the heirs; the Court of Appeal continued to affirm the lower court's opinion that the whole question of whether Mellerio's death was accident or suicide was irrelevant to the issues of the case, since even if the heirs could prove their most damaging insinuations on this point, the worst they could do would be to demonstrate that Mellerio had died in a fit of madness. Even if such an allegation were true, it would concern an event that had occurred some seven months after the drawing up of the last of the testaments in question. But since the police report throws new light on an aspect of the case that does figure so largely in Browning's version of the case, the public prosecutor's discussion of Mellerio's death is given below in full:

> As for Antonio's death, Mme Debacker has maintained that it was an accident; the heirs have claimed it was suicide. It should be noted that they do not claim deliberate suicide, but rather that in the grip of a religious frenzy Antonio thought he heard his mother and the angels calling him, and threw himself off the belvedere to fly to them.
>
> On this point there are no witnesses of any kind. In their latest brief the heirs asked for an examination of the police report made at the time of the first suspicion of suicide.
>
> The Public Prosecutor has agreed to their request. The

165

ROUGH IN BRUTAL PRINT

first of the documents in this report is an unimportant letter from the commissioner of police, dated 13 April 1870 [the date of Mellerio's death], containing nothing more than a description of the event; it does, however, refer to suicide. Then comes the police report itself, of the same date, composed of the following depositions:

1) *Richer*, the gardener, attested that at 10 A.M., while working in the park about 60 meters from the château, he heard a thud and then saw in the garden walk the body of Mellerio, whose skull was cracked; he thought Mellerio probably fell accidentally. Dr. Laurent was summoned; he determined that death had been instantaneous. The witness added that for some time Mellerio had been a little disturbed in his head, and had been subject to fits of mental derangement;

2) *Marse*, day laborer, gave the same testimony;

3) *Boucher*, servant, attested that at 9:45 A.M. Mellerio had ordered him to harness a horse, that he had done so; that then Richer came to tell him that Mellerio had just fallen and killed himself. He added that for some time Mellerio had been subject to fits of mental derangement.

That is all the information gathered by the police, and the only conclusion the heirs can draw from it would be that it was possible for public opinion to be convinced that Mellerio had suffered from fits of mental derangement.

We have here, in effect, a sort of commission of inquiry held right on the scene, from which it is possible to infer some fits of derangement in the last days of Mellerio's life, but not to find the slightest trace of continuous madness—though it is quite possible that these symptoms might have been precursors of a later attack of insanity.

The crucial question, of course, concerns the circumstances under which the testaments, particularly the last testament, of 21 October 1869, were drawn up. In approaching his final consideration of this question, M. Delise offers in passing an acute observation on the heirs' allegation that Mellerio's gift to Mme Debacker in 1868 of a 12,000 franc annuity was nothing more than an effort to rid himself of her while absolving himself of financial responsibility. "But the contents of this document, which is authentic and unchallengeable, both on account of its early date and on account of its precise legal terminology, demonstrate the contrary, because this income is made payable to Mme Debacker either at Paris or at *TAILLEVILLE*. Now, if Mme

Debacker were to receive her income at Tailleville, it must be because she would be continuing to live with Mellerio. In this act, then, M. Mellerio's only intention can have been to guarantee the independence of Mme Debacker."

As for the essential document, the testament of 21 October 1869, M. Delise finds that both Mellerio's clarity of mind and his fixed and persistent intentions are unmistakably displayed in the famous letter to Maître Prevost of 10 August 1869. Since this letter is so fatally damaging to the heirs' case, M. Delise takes their recourse to charges that it was forged to be a tactic as despicable as it is patently false. He concludes his address to the court:

> The evidence before the Court is irrefutable, as the Mellerio heirs well understood; and since their position on these grounds was untenable, they have hit on a new approach by denying the authenticity of the handwriting of the letter from Mellerio to Prevost. And since that handwriting was the same as that of the two testaments, they are likewise compelled to deny the authenticity of the testaments as well. The Court is baffled by their new procedure, however, since although their intention is clearly to raise doubts as to the authenticity of these documents, their filed list of allegations nowhere specifically states a denial of that authenticity.

After scornfully dismissing the various efforts by the heirs to impugn the handwriting of the documents in question ("As for the argument of the heirs based on the *cedilles* below Mellerio's 'c's,' the public prosecutor will not even discuss that"), M. Delise exposes the most fatuous implications of these new charges.

> The arguments of the heirs are in fact inherently incompatible. Mme Debacker is accused of forgery and undue influence, but forgery and undue influence are actually contradictory. After all, if Mme Debacker could exert undue influence, why should she bother with forgery? Nor, according to the heirs' line of argument, was Mme Debacker very intelligent, if she indulged in an absurd imprudence by inviting Prevost to come to Tailleville to consult with Mellerio. Furthermore, since M. Hébert was a party to this invitation, he too must necessarily be alleged to have been an accomplice of the forger. These charges cannot be taken seriously—they rebound against those who have brought them, and what they prove is that the heirs' case is desperate.

According to the public prosecutor, the conclusion is obvious. "The testament of 21 October 1869 was drawn up after considerable reflection and after taking into account the counsel of several advisers. This fact in itself is sufficient to win the case for the defendants." The justice of the case is so clear, in fact, that M. Delise cannot resist in his closing remarks a few words of reproach to the Mellerio heirs for their brazenness in having brought the suit in the first place, let alone having persisted in an appeal:

> The Public Prosecutor wishes to add a few words on the subject of the requested commission of inquiry. Touching lightly on the large number of allegations that are totally irrelevant to the suit, he remarks that in the course of the original trial the heirs themselves retracted the allegations of undue influence relating to the Convent of la Délivrande, which proves the frivolity [*la légèreté*] of their having included them in the first place. He further remarks that as for the original allegations, they were examined and rightly rejected by the lower Court, since they are radically flawed, in that they are nothing but a paraphrase of the Jousse affidavit and are therefore highly suspect. As for the new allegations, there are two observations to be made about them: first, that they all deal with acts of mental derangement, none with undue influence; second, that the vagueness of their dating tends to suggest deliberate policy on the part of the heirs, and besides, they relate only to the the last month of 1869 and the early part of 1870, being nothing more than a confirmation of the original police report.
>
> In fact, going further still, it must be said, considering the method whereby the last testament was drawn up, that even if any such acts of derangement at that time could be proved before the Court, there would still be no good cause for ordering a commission of inquiry.
>
> These, says the Public Prosecutor, are our conclusions. It is not for us to decide if Mellerio did well, or if he ought rather to have followed the advice of M. Prevost—that issue does not fall within the province of our duty. The question before this Court is to decide whether or not the testator was completely competent and independent. He was. Therefore, his testament must be honored.

In its formal decision the Court of Appeal completely concurred with the public prosecutor. After reviewing all the key evidence and arguments of the case, it "affirm[ed] the judgment here being appealed," and "order[ed] the appellants to pay the original fine and all costs."

THE 1874 APPEAL

Having lost their 1873 appeal of the 1872 judgment, the Mellerio heirs in 1874 took their case to the Cour de Cassation, the French equivalent of the Supreme Court for matters of private law, as the Conseil d'Etat is for public law. "In French legal theory, the function of the Cour de Cassation is limited to cassation—that is, setting aside judgments for errors of law appearing in the opinion of the court below, and referring the case for final determination to an appellate court other than that which rendered the decision" (David and de Vries, *The French Legal System*, p. 35). These decisions by the Cour de Cassation are made by a panel of at least nine judges.

It should be noted that an appeal to the Cour de Cassation must be made entirely on grounds of error in law by the Court of Appeal. Consequently, the 1874 argument of the Mellerio heirs consisted of three charges:

1. The heirs charged that the Court of Appeal had violated Articles 141 and 170 of the Code of Civil Procedure, in that its decision did not directly address the heirs' allegations that the disputed testament was not the work of Antonio Mellerio. In considering this charge, the Cour de Cassation found that it follows "from the text itself of the document produced in support of the appeal, dated 26 May 1873 and entitled Explicatory Note, that the Mellerio heirs did in fact not make any formal allegations aimed at having the testament of 21 October 1869 declared to be not the testament of Antonio Mellerio; that therefore this charge is without basis in fact."

2. The heirs charged that the Court of Appeal had improperly applied Article 173 of the Code of Civil Procedure, and had "confounded a substantive issue with a simple question of procedure," when it decided that charges of forgery would constitute entirely new grounds of argument and hence were not admissible in an appeal. In considering this charge, the Cour de Cassation found that "in the absence of formal allegations relevant to the handwriting of the disputed testament, the judges of the lower Court [of Appeal] could not have been required to rule, nor did they rule on [this] question."

3. And finally the heirs charged that the Court of Appeal had improperly applied Articles 1338 and 1340 of the Code of Civil Procedure, in its decision that charges of forgery were inadmissible in an appeal because the original suit for nullification of the disputed testament on grounds of unsoundness of mind and exertion of undue influence "constituted, as far as the authenticity of the documents is concerned, an admission equivalent to an express declaration." On this charge, the Cour de Cassation found that the appellate judges had merely "confined themselves to the facts of the case and restricted themselves to applying the inferences derived therefrom to each party's respective suit."

The Cour de Cassation denied the Mellerio heirs' appeal. After their third defeat, there was no further recourse available. On 18 August 1874, more than four years after Antonio Mellerio's death, Mme Debacker and the convent of la Délivrande took clear title to his estate.

THE MELLERIO FAMILY HISTORY

It is perhaps fitting, given their complete failure to have their own way in court, that the Mellerio heirs at least be given the satisfaction of having the last word. In 1893, nineteen years after the rejection of their final appeal, a history of the Mellerio family was privately printed by the same Joseph Mellerio who had been one of the plaintiffs against Mme Debacker. In this long celebration of the Mellerios' accumulated wealth and social connections, the subject of Antonio Mellerio's career is so obviously distasteful to Joseph that he does not linger over it, nor does his terse account exactly match that of the court records. But it does provide an appropriate, if slightly biased, closing flourish to the story.

> . . . Jean-Antoine [Antonio's father], born in 1798, [was] known to us as Uncle Tony. He followed his uncle Jean-Baptiste (Mylord), as a jeweler at 22 Rue Vivienne: "Mellerio-Meller, at the sign of the Iron Crown."
> Later, Uncle Tony moved his shop to 1 Quai d'Orsay, on the second floor, keeping the name "Mellerio-Meller."
> He married a Mlle Jelpo, from Switzerland.
> The younger Mlle Jelpo married M. Baudry, who had property at Arnouville.
> Their daughter married M. Forcade, a well-to-do wine

170

merchant of Bordeaux. [This daughter was Louise Fortunée, also a plaintiff in the suit. M. Forcade was the coexecutor of Mellerio's testament (pp. 57, 65).]

Uncle Tony became very wealthy.

He had three children—a girl and two boys.

The girl died in infancy.

The older son, Antonio, born in 1827, grew up to be a very handsome man. He was blond and resembled his mother, who spoiled him totally.

He was educated at a Protestant boarding school, without religious principles—a circumstance at which the family were especially surprised since they regularly observed Uncle Tony's wife at mass at the church of Saint-Roche.

Antonio became a dandy [un dandy]. His mother gave him an enormous allowance, with the result that he threw himself into fashionable pleasures and dissipations, in company with the young rakes of the Epoque.

He became involved with a courtesan [une femme galante] named Anna, whose married name was Debacker. She succeeded in getting him into her clutches, and never let him escape.

She took advantage of the poor boy's mental derangement to have herself named his sole legatee, and all Uncle Tony's fortune was devoured by this adventuress, to the detriment of the family, who brought suit to no avail.

The second son, Victor, born in 1830, was raised with the same lack of principles as his brother, at that same Protestant school. He endeavored to imitate his brother in debauchery, but his health would not permit it. He died at twenty-five, completely exhausted [totalement usé].

He too was a handsome boy, tall and dark, very intelligent, very kindhearted—he would have made an excellent merchant. Before his own death [in 1860], Uncle Tony had ample time to contemplate the results of the immoral education he had given his sons. May this sad tale serve as an example to us all!

His wife died suddenly one night at the dinner table, with no one by her side but an old clerk, a little hunchback named Morel.

There remains no trace of this unhappy branch of the family—it has entirely disappeared.

(From Joseph Mellerio, *The Mellerio Family: Its Origins and History* [privately printed by Dumoulin and Company: Paris, 1893], pp. 151–53.)

Appendix

This appendix contains a collection of several other pieces of information, from both documentary and oral sources, acquired in the process of obtaining the source material of Browning's poem. Included here are brief reports of two other concurrent lawsuits—both successful—in which the Mellerio family was then engaged; branches of the Mellerio family tree; some corrections and amplifications of the list, given by Browning to Mrs. Orr for her *Handbook*, of original names corresponding to the pseudonyms used in the published poem; and the history of the château of Tailleville from Mme Debacker's occupation up to the present day. Like the last part of book 12 of *The Ring and the Book*, the information in this Appendix gives "the final state o' the story" (*Ring*, 12.823).

CONCURRENT LAWSUITS

PARIS (First Chamber), 3 June 1872

Mellerio v. Isabel de Bourbon

19 March 1872, judgment of the Civil Court of the Seine (First Chamber), as follows:

"The Court, considering that the former Queen of Spain, Dona Isabel de Bourbon, and Don François d'Assise de Bourbon, authorizing her [to appear before the Court], in the suit brought by the Mellerio brothers for payment for jewelry furnished by them, claim that the Court does not have personal or subject matter jurisdiction in this case; considering that every French citizen has the right to resort to the courts of his country for justice; that this right, which derives from the protection owed to a citizen by his government, is plainly stated in Article 14 of the Civil Code, according to which a foreign national may be sued in a French court for breach of contracts made by him with French persons, even if such contracts were entered into in foreign countries; that there are no exceptions to this statute, except those specifically established by French law or by principles of international law; considering that if it is established that the Mellerio brothers—whose firm is located in Paris, 9 rue de la Paix— are French citizens, and if Dona Isabel de Bourbon did in fact contract with them, either in France or abroad, they therefore may bring suit, in the Court of the Seine, against the defendants, who reside in Paris; considering that, on the first point, the Mellerio brothers have submitted ample evidence to demonstrate their French nationality; that it is irrelevant that Dona Isabel was unaware of this fact, because it is the responsibility of each party to a contract to determine the nationality of the persons he contracts with;

Considering that there is no question whatever that the defendant ordered the creation and delivery of the various pieces of jewelry from the Mellerio brothers, that she does not deny having received those pieces, some in Paris and some in Madrid, and that she had placed part of the order at the main office of the Mellerios in the rue de la Paix and part at the branch in Madrid, which is managed by a representative of the Mellerio brothers; that, therefore, to claim that the Court does not have jurisdiction would require the former Queen of Spain to demonstrate that she bought the jewelry whose cost is the subject of this dispute in her capacity as sovereign, at the expense of the Spanish treasury, which, according to this line of reasoning, would then be solely responsible for the debt owed to the Mellerio brothers; considering that this claim, far from being supported by the *evidence* of the case, is inconsistent with it; that in fact it has been made clear that the jewelry whose cost is the subject of this dispute was furnished to the former Queen of Spain either for her own personal use or for gifts intended for various persons, particularly for her daughter, the Princess de Girgenti, on the occasion of her marriage; that, moreover, deliveries of jewelry were made after as well as before the Spanish revolution of September 1868, and that a large portion of the jewelry was then delivered in Paris, in the same manner and to the same private servants of the former Queen; that it cannot therefore be reasonably argued that this jewelry was sold to the government of Spain; considering, moreover, that the Spanish treasury does not possess any crown jewels, according to the Spanish Law of 12 May 1865, which, in its list of public property available for the sovereign's personal use, makes no mention of any crown jewelry; considering, accordingly, that the contract between the Mellerio brothers and the former Queen of Spain must therefore be treated as a matter involving only private interests, subject not to the principles of the law of nations but rather to the principles of French civil law; from which the conclusion is to be drawn that the Mellerio brothers did have the right to bring suit in the Court of the Seine, according to Article 14 of the Civil Code; on these grounds, declares that it has jurisdiction over the persons and the case[, and renders judgment in favor of the plaintiffs].

Appeal [in which this judgment was affirmed].

(From *Pandectes Chronologiques*, Vol. 5 [1870–77], Part 2, p. 68.)

Paris, 9 February 1874

(Mellerio v. Delaporte and Sommier)

[Headnote]

The Mellerio brothers, jewelers, sold to M. A. Sommier in 1868 various pieces of jewelry for the sum of 28, 681 francs, 50 centimes. Shortly thereafter, the mother of M. Sommier placed an announcement in the newspapers that she had filed a request for a legal guardian for her son, age twenty-two. On 23 April 1869 M. Delaporte was appointed legal guardian of M. A. Sommier. MM. Mellerio thereupon claimed the balance of the monies owed them. M. Delaporte, without denying that M. Sommier had bought the jewelry, claimed that the purchases were subject to the legal measures taken by the family, on account of the unconscionability of the contract [(*il*) *en critiquait l'exagération*]. Being of the opinion that the plaintiffs were not absolutely entitled to the full amount of the debt owed them, he offered them 15,000 francs.

On 27 November 1872 the Civil Court of the Seine handed down the following judgment: "Considering that the Mellerio brothers claim from Sommier, and from Delaporte, his legal guardian, the sum of 28,681 francs, 50 centimes, for jewelry sold to Sommier in 1868; considering that, setting to one side the question as to whether Sommier, who is now provided with a legal guardian, ought not to have bought that jewelry, the Court does have the necessary information to make an accurate estimate of the money owed to the Mellerio brothers; considering that Delaporte, in his capacity as legal guardian, has already paid the Mellerio brothers the sum of 15,000 francs, and that he is prepared to pay a further sum of 5,000 francs in full settlement; considering that the documents of the case have demonstrated that this sum would be a sufficient payment for the articles in question, taking into consideration the conditions and circumstances under which they were sold; on these grounds, the Court orders Sommier and Delaporte, in his capacity as guardian, to pay the Mellerios the sum of 5,000 francs, in full settlement, with interest from the day of filing suit.

Appeal by the Mellerio brothers.

Decision [of the Court of Appeal of Paris]

The Court, Considering that Delaporte, the legal guardian of M. Sommier, disputes neither the integrity of the Mellerio brothers, nor the accuracy of the list of items in their bill, nor their prices; that he limits himself to maintaining that the Mellerios took advantage of Sommier's wealth to sell him an unreasonably large amount of jewelry, and that he is willing to settle for 20,000 francs;

But considering that, whatever may have been the regrettable facility with which this jewelry was sold to a youth only twenty-two years old, it is nevertheless uncontested that the sale was made; that on the dates of sale of the various pieces of jewelry Sommier was of full age, in possession of all his rights and commanding a fortune of considerable size; that the judgment appointing a legal guardian for him is dated 28 August 1869, later by several months than the date of the last sale; that, according to Article 502 of the Civil Code, the appointment of a legal guardian is effective only from the date of the judgment by which he is appointed; on these grounds, sets aside the judgment here being appealed, wherein the first judges ordered a settlement of only 5000 francs, plus interest from the day of filing suit; orders Sommier and Delaporte, in his capacity as legal guardian, to pay the appellants, over and above the sum required by the original judgment, the sum of 8,778 francs, 50 centimes.

9 February 1874—Court of Paris, Messieurs Brière-Valigny, President; Dherbelot, Deputy Public Prosecutor; Debacq and Carraby, Counsels.

(From *Recueil Général des Lois et des Arrêts* [Sirey: Paris, 1874], p. 200.)

THE MELLERIO FAMILY TREE

The chart opposite, assembled from portions of Joseph Mellerio's family history, the pleadings and briefs of the Debacker lawsuits, and various scattered references in the

Branches of the Mellerio Family Tree

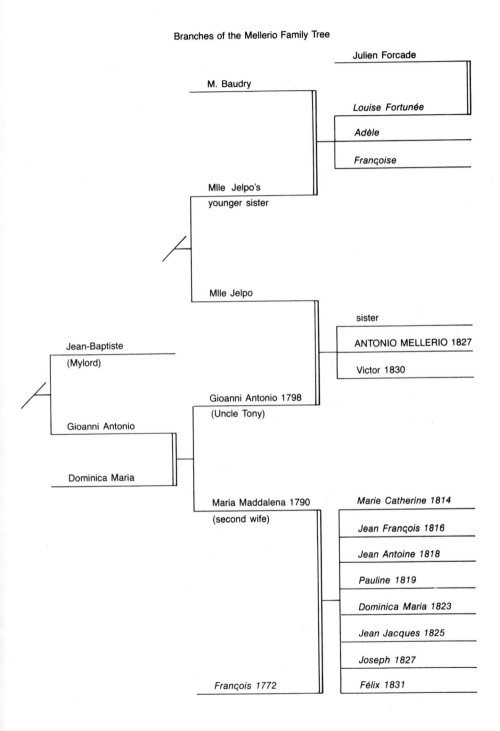

newspaper accounts of those suits, provides a view of the
family relationships between Antonio Mellerio and the relatives who contested his testament. Those names in italics,
toward the right, are the ten plaintiffs, who are mentioned in
Browning's poem only as an "uncertain sort of Cousinry"
(1.772). They are, in fact, all first cousins of Antonio: seven
(toward the bottom) are the children of Antonio's father's
sister, Maria Maddalena, and three (toward the top) are the
children of Antonio's mother's sister, the younger Mlle
Jelpo. The only cousin missing from the list of plaintiffs is
Jean Jacques, who had died before the case came to court
(there is a reference in the 1872 trial to Antonio's generosity
toward "Jacques's widow," p. 75).

It is not clear from the chart just why Browning refers to
these relationships as "uncertain." The only reason suggested by the genealogy is that since Maria Maddalena was
only the second wife of François Mellerio, perhaps she was
not the mother of all the children attributed to her marriage
to François. But since the family history is an extremely
detailed document, if any of these eight children had come
from the first wife, she ought certainly to have been mentioned somewhere, and she is not. Perhaps Browning's description simply reflects his own vagueness as to the exact
relationships involved. At any rate, the epithet "uncertain"
was undoubtedly useful to him, even if apparently not
entirely deserved, as an insinuation that the plaintiffs were
so remotely connected to Antonio that their suit was not
even justified by close legal family ties.

The descendants of Jean François still maintain the same
flourishing jewelry business, still at the same address, 9 rue
de la Paix, next door to Cartier's. Joseph Mellerio's family
history was obtained there from one François Mellerio, born
in 1943, the great-great-grandson of Jean François, and thus
Antonio's first cousin, four times removed.

ADDENDA TO LIST OF PUBLISHED PSEUDONYMS

In his original version of *Red Cotton Night-Cap Country*,
Browning had reinforced his impression of strict historical
factuality by using the real names of the people and places
involved in the scandal. However, as he wrote in a letter to T.
J. Nettleship, dated 16 May 1889, his attorney later persuaded

him to substitute pseudonyms: "Indeed the facts are so exactly put down, that, in order to avoid the possibility of prosecution for Libel—that is, telling the exact truth—I changed all the names of persons and places, as they stood in the original 'Proofs' and gave them as they are to be found in Mrs. Orr's *Handbook*" (*Letters*, ed. Hood, p. 309). This list, provided by Browning for Mrs. Orr, is reproduced in Charlotte Porter and Helen A. Clarke's Florentine Edition, Vol. 10. But by comparing the poem with its source material, and also with a holograph manuscript in the Balliol College library at Oxford (Balliol MS. 388), it is possible to make that list of altered factual details a little more complete and, in a few instances, a little more accurate. There are eleven new entries to be added; following the practice of Mrs. Orr and Misses Porter and Clarke, they are arranged below according to the line number of their first appearance in the published poem. The published version, in italics, is followed by the original, in roman.

1.437 *two miles far*: four miles far
    (the distance from Tailleville to la Délivrande)

1.632 *by birth a Madrilene*: by birth a Turinese
    (referring to Mellerio's father)

1.785 *Firm-Miranda, London and New-York*
    Mellerio Brothers—Meller, people say.
    (Mrs. Orr and the Florentine Edition do provide this information, but without comment. François Mellerio explained that the name had been changed to "Meller" during the French Revolution, when nationalist sentiment made it dangerous to be a foreigner in France. The original name was subsequently restored.)

2.628–30 *Clara de Millefleurs, of the noble race,*
    Was Lucie Steiner, child to Dominique
    And Magdalen Commercy . . .
    Anna de Beaupré, of the noble race,
    Was Sophy Trayer, child to Dominic
    And Magdalen Lalory . . .
    (The Florentine editors give no Christian names for the parents, and misspell the original family names

as "Mayer" and "Larocy." Browning left unaltered
the Christian names of the parents, except for the
spelling of the father's.)

2.637 *Monsieur Ulysse Mulhausen, young and smart*
Monsieur Achille Debacker, young and brisk

(referring to Mme Debacker's husband)

2.857 *Gustave:* Alfred

(referring to M. Debacker's trade name)

3.523 *Steiner, Mulhausen, whatsoe'er your name*

Trayer, Betrayer, whatsoe'er your name

(As in the play on *Délivrande*—Delivering Virgin
[2.155], the introduction of pseudonyms here, in
this sneer of the cousinry's at Mme Debacker, involves the loss of another opportunity for double
meaning. See pp. 144–45.)

3.781 *Milsand, who makest warm my wintry world*

O Friend, who makest warm my wintry world

(Here is the unique instance, in the progression
from the Balliol manuscript to the published version, of Browning's altering the text of his draft to
provide a true name in his publication. The inclusion of the real name of Milsand, one of Browning's
oldest and best friends, can be perceived as rather a
touching compliment to their relationship, as if
Browning, in the course of reluctantly distancing
his poem from the literal detail so important to it,
here came across a single possibility of affirming at
least one direct and personal link between his poem
and the real world.

4.243 *Count Mailleville built yon church.*

Count Baldwin built yon church.

(Mellerio, on the belvedere, addresses the Virgin of
la Délivrande).

In addition there are two places in the poem where Browning in his revision failed to eliminate completely all traces of
the original names. First, Mellerio's conviction that the
name of the local church derived "From the Delivering Virgin, niched and known" (2.155) makes sense as an example

of his simplemindedness in matters of faith only if the name of the church is "la Délivrande." There is really no way such a derivation as "Delivering Virgin" could be "A pious rendering of Rare Vissante, / The proper name which erst our province bore" (2.158–59; for a full discussion of this point, see pp. 144–45). And second, although everywhere else in the poem "Caen" was renamed "Vire," the news of the death of Mellerio's mother is still sent by telegraph to "Caen," (3.191) and Mellerio then travels to her deathbed in Paris from "Caen" (3.196).

RECENT HISTORY OF THE CHÂTEAU OF TAILLEVILLE

In the town records of Tailleville are listed the deaths of "Mellerio, Antonio, 10 a.m., 13 April 1870," and "Trayer, Anna Sophie, 5 a.m., 22 May 1887, en château." According to M. Pierre, who has been the mayor of Tailleville since 1930, the convent wished to sell the property when they first took possession of it after Mme Debacker's death, but since they were unwilling at that time to submit to a complete inventory of the estate, as they would have been required to do by the Napoleonic laws of their founding, they decided to rent it out instead. From 1890, for the next forty-five years, the house was inhabited by a succession of the mayors of Tailleville—M. Price, from 1890 to 1900; M. Offret, from 1901 to 1929; and M. Pierre from 1930 to 1944. During World War II the château was commandeered to serve as the Nazi headquarters for the region. Located only one kilometer from the English Channel, it was a key unit in the German line of fortification, and was named Fort Hildendorff, after the German general. At first, in 1941, the Nazis merely established a radar unit in the château, leaving M. Pierre a small corner for himself; but in 1943 they began an intensive occupation that displaced M. Pierre entirely, mining the park and building an elaborate system of seventeen blockhouses and innumerable tunnels around the château.

Since Fort Hildendorff was never attacked, it was undamaged by the war, except that the absence of all maintenance, especially to the roof, had led to a state of disrepair that deteriorated every year until the château reached the point of near collapse. In 1973 it was acquired by the *Chiffoniers d'Emmaüs* (a society roughly equivalent to Goodwill Industries), who repaired the ravages of time and the Nazis, and made the château habitable once again. It is currently in use as the central office of their organization, housing between thirty and thirty-five residents. Although apparently destined never to be a hospital, it has been saved from destruction, and finally, more than one hundred years after his death, it has come to serve a charitable purpose at least similar to that which Antonio Mellerio stipulated in his disputed testament.

Notes

CHAPTER ONE

1. See, for instance, in a letter to Isabella Blagden, 19 August 1865, Browning's reference to "my great venture, the murder-poem, which I do hope will strike you and all good lovers of mine," and his remark to Fields, Osgood (the American publishers), 19 July 1867, that for all its 20,000 lines "it is the shortest poem, for the stuff in it, I ever wrote" (*Letters of Robert Browning, Collected by Thomas J. Wise*, ed. Thurman L. Hood [New Haven, Conn.: Yale University Press, 1933], pp. 90, 114).

2. Robert Browning, *The Ring and the Book*, Florentine Edition, vol. 6, ed. Charlotte Porter and Helen A. Clarke (New York: Thomas Y. Crowell, 1898), 1.34. All citations from Browning in this study, including those from *Red Cotton Night-Cap Country* (vol. 10), will be taken from this edition.

3. Charles W. Hodell, *The Old Yellow Book: Source of Browning's "The Ring and the Book"* (Carnegie Institute of Washington, 1908), and John Marshall Gest, *The Old Yellow Book: Source of Browning's "The Ring and the Book"* (Philadelphia: University of Pennsylvania Press, 1927).

4. A. K. Cook, *A Commentary upon Browning's "The Ring and the Book"* (London: Oxford University Press, 1920), p. 293.

5. Philip Drew, *The Poetry of Browning: A Critical Introduction* (London: Methuen, 1970), p. 327.

6. Alfred Domett, quoted in Clyde de L. Ryals, *Browning's Later Poetry, 1871–1889* (Ithaca, N.Y.: Cornell University Press, 1975), p. 83.

7. *Harper's Monthly Magazine* 42 (August 1873):461.

8. G. A. Simcox, in *The Academy* 4 (2 June 1873):203.

9. Anonymous review, *British Quarterly Review* 58 (1 July 1873):241.

10. William Dean Howells, in *Atlantic Monthly* 32 (July 1873):115.

11. G. K. Chesterton, *Robert Browning* (London: MacMillan, 1903), pp. 122–23.

12. *Robert Browning and Julia Wedgwood: A Broken Friendship As Revealed by Their Letters*, ed. Richard Curl (New York: Frederick A. Stoker, 1937), 19 November 1868, pp. 143–44.

13. Beatrice Corrigan, *Curious Annals: New Documents Relating to Browning's Roman Murder Story* (Toronto: University of Toronto Press, 1971).

14. Rene David and Henry P. de Vries, *The French Legal System* (New York: Oceana, 1958), p. 36.

CHAPTER FIVE

1. *New Letters of Robert Browning*, ed. William Clyde DeVane and Kenneth Leslie Knickerbocker (New Haven, Conn.: Yale University Press, 1950), p. 211 n. 2.

2. In this vein Clyde de L. Ryals also sees this poem as an instance of "a record of a quest, a distance traveled and a goal reached," focusing "on a central question of self-identity" (*Browning's Later Poetry, 1871–1889* [Ithaca, N.Y.: Cornell University Press, 1975], pp. 83–84).

3. The quotation from Richer comes from the police report made on the spot, as quoted in the newspaper account of 1873. It was not found in any 1872 newspaper in the *Archives*, but since Browning deals directly with this material in his poem, it can reasonably be supposed that this report was among the "legal documents" procured for him by Milsand (for the full text of the relevant portion of this letter to Nettleship, see the Introduction, p. 16). Perhaps, however, this section of the poem is only an instance of the "guess at something equivalent" mentioned in the "Advertisement" given on p. 3), not a deliberate distortion.

4. When quoting from *Red Cotton Night-Cap Country*, for the sake of consistency I have retained the original names of the characters and places involved.

5. G. Burnel, *Notre Dame de la Dell'yvrande* (n.p., 1972), pp. 51–52. This pamphlet, giving the history of the sacred site from pagan times, was published to commemorate the hundreth anniversary of the crowning of the statue of the Virgin of la Délivrande, a ceremony that figures dramatically in Browning's poem—see, for instance, ll. 423–531.

6. Florentine Edition, 11:1.

7. Charlotte Porter and Helen A. Clarke, in their notes to the Florentine Edition of Browning, 10:300.

8. William Clyde DeVane, *Browning's "Parleyings": The Autobiography of a Mind* (New Haven, Conn.: Yale University Press, 1927), chap. 1.

Index

185